Dedication

This book is dedicated to my three lovely grandchildren: Lydia and Tegan who sadly lost their angel of a mum, Sarah, their anchor in life's ocean, and my grandson, Cody, our wonderful new kid on the block.

I sincerely hope these three will keep the traditions and the memories of the old Romanies alive in their tiny hearts to hand down to their children and inspire in them the Romany culture.

Custi Chavies.

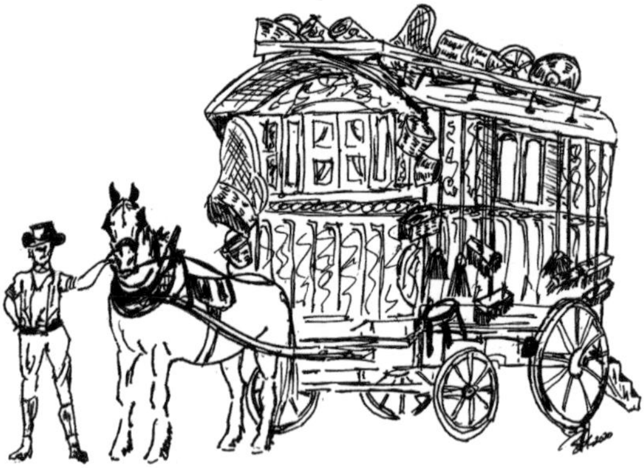

BRUSH WAGON

As I went up North, I saw old West,
I saw him following on;
Then my eyes came down to rest,
On a brand new Brush Wagon.

It was being pulled by a big grey mare,
As big as a passing cloud,
And on the front was driving her,
Old Grypher West so proud.

I shouted to my pal Grypher,
'Do you not think that I am blunt,
But why are you driving there
With your wagon back to front?'

'That is the way the wagon was made,'
Old Grypher called to me,
'So just pull up into the shade
And we will make a pot of tea.'

Contents

Preface 1

Introduction (or Genesis) 4
The Windy City 9
Rust, Gunners & Tats 17
My Fair Lady & Other Folk 22
Albert Lamb & Other Good People 33
The Dealing Life 41
Aunt Milly Hudson and Tater Billy 45
A Roadside Reverie 49
A Couple Of Lessons In Dealing 58
And Did Those Hooves... 63
A Turkey Tale 67
A Riot Of Romanies 69
The Art Of The Deal 75
Out On The Knocker 93
Stalham Sale 102
Bonney Price 109
Life On The Drom 111
Come Buy My Wares! 132
Crafty Folk & Cannon Balls 139
Romany Ways And Vardoes 146
North Walsham All-Sorts 154
Some Closing Words 166

Glossary 168
Acknowledgements 182
About the author 184

Mike Harmer standing at the gates to the yard once known as The Windy City

Preface

You may know North Walsham, a small unassuming market town located near the top right corner of that bulge into the North Sea we know as Norfolk. Its main, and most recent, claim to fame is as the site of the last battle of the Peasant's Revolt back in 1381.

On the outskirts of the town there is a deceptively leafy lane that heads east. This is Marshgate and if, on a Sunday morning, you were to walk past the short row of houses that give way to fields on one side and the hidden hinterlands of industrialisation on the other, you would eventually reach the turning into Mike Harmer's reclamation yard. The entrance is marked by the two tall wrought-iron gates that originally graced Randell's foundry at St Nicholas Works on a site now occupied by Sainsbury's in the nearby town. Like virtually everything you will find here, these gates are a part of Norfolk's past. On your right, as you walk on up the drive, your eyes will be drawn to the treasures lurking in the long grass, half-covered by sprawling weeds. There are chimney pots, fireplaces, galvanised buckets, even old bits of agricultural machinery, all awaiting the opportunity to be resurrected for some functional or decorative purpose. Ahead of you, dotted all around, lie stacks of building materials reclaimed from everywhere and anywhere; from ramshackle outbuildings to the most prestigious country piles: paments, Norfolk reds, ridge tiles, pan tiles and mammoth wooden beams. It is, in every sense, a reclamation yard; a conduit through which Norfolk's unwanted and abandoned past is funnelled to be given a new lease of life.

At the far end, past the shepherd's hut, a door leads into the carpentry workshop where Mike's son, Rod, carries on his business during the week. However on Sunday mornings this space is reserved for Mike's meetings - affectionately known as the grumpy old men's club. You will see him across the way as you enter, perched on his stool beyond the workbench. Beside him stands a curiously steampunk wood-burning stove fashioned from an old water boiler with a snaking flue that wends its way through the canopy of cobwebs. As likely as not, Mike will be in full toothless flow recounting one of his tales to whoever has gathered there today. Some tales have almost worn smooth with the telling while others are still undergoing the process of refinement. In this, the second of his memoirs, you are offered a ringside seat as a motley crew tumble by with their idiosyncrasies and eccentric ways. In his inimitable manner, Mike offers his own perspective on his Romany heritage and reveals a series of insights into his life as a dealer in scrap and antiques.

Over a century has gone by since Mike's maternal Romany grandparents had their horses requisitioned into the war effort. They used the payment to buy a parcel of land and cease their nomadic ways. The twentieth century was marginalising their way of life. And so it went on, with his Romany mother marrying his Gorgio[1] father, continuing the process of assimilation. In some ways, Mike can appear more rooted than many of us. He lives on the same patch of land that housed him as a boy, though the railway carriages that once stood there have been replaced by a house composed of reclaimed materials, a hidden museum to Norfolk's history. But despite this there is something intrinsically 'gypsy' about him. He is a rover, uncomfortable if he is kept cooped up. The reality of the Romany way of life contrasts with the romantic view of the wandering vagabond. The nomadic lifestyle was primarily the sound economic approach to finding the casual seasonal agricultural work among a group of people who saw themselves as set apart from their sedentary counterparts. The different Romany families - clans, if you will - all had their shared territories and Mike's grandparents were primarily Norfolk based. Mike continues the tradition. For the best part of eighty years he has been travelling the same byways in search of deals and throughout that time he has been simultaneously gathering a folk history of the area, one composed of the stories of the people. It

---

1   Gorgio: Romany word for 'Non-Romany'

is as if the towns and villages serve as Mike's memory palace. You have only to mention a placename to him and, as likely as not, he will be able to retrieve a tale associated with it: a person he met, or some mishap he had heard about. He really has a prodigious memory and he is keen to share this knowledge before it is lost.

So let us say that this book represents yet another corner in his reclamation yard, where the lives of many have been reclaimed from obscurity and been given the opportunity to extend their days to be enjoyed by future generations.

Nick White
The Old Vicarage, Bacton

Introduction (or Genesis)

Hello, readers. It's me, back again – old Mike Harmer. Several old boys have asked if I would do another book. I must be mad or plain *divvy* (silly): this book writing is bloody hard. I am not yet into computers and I am still writing like Shakespeare, with a pen. So I was very happy when I thought I had finally finished and could have a well-deserved cuppa but my friend Nick White, who I would describe as my editor, pressed me to write a little more about my early childhood by way of introduction. So, with a deep breath and aching fingers I picked up the pen again to scribble out my opening gospel. I suppose we can call it Genesis.

I think I have told you readers how I was raised, if that is the right word, and brought up in a railway carriage. The only small blip in my delightful early life, was when I was about five years old. Most of my family thought my sudden illness was brought on by me eating dirty pig potatoes from an equally dirty outside copper, which my father, Edgie, would use to boil potatoes for his pigs. It seems Edgie and me would eat these straight from the copper.

But what happened is that I started to feel a little gammy, a word often used here in Norfolk, it means to feel unwell. My mother got a *crocus* (an old Romany word for a doctor) to have a look at me. I don't know who he was, probably a local witch-doctor. He told my mother, "He's alright. Keep taking the pills," and he pissed off.

Anyway, poor little Mike Harmer got a great deal worse, so in came a better *crocus*. He gave me the full SP and told mother, "This boy has meningitis. and I don't think he will survive through the night".

What a thing to say! How dare he! No more sherbets! No more gobstoppers! Somehow I must've heard the old *crocus*. Christ, I hadn't any intention to pack it all in I wanted to get older. I wanted to wear long trousers. I wanted to climb trees!

So they rushed me to Norwich's Jenny Lind hospital and, against all odds, I somehow survived. I was in the hospital for several weeks, then they moved me down to Cromer-on-Sea into a convalescent hospital. Hang on readers, I can feel a tale coming on.

Most days down at this hospital in Cromer, a nurse would take a group of us to get some of that bracing sea air into our lungs. Off down the road we would go: seven or eight of us youngsters following Mary Poppins pushing a large old pram with two small chavies (children) in it. I remember one sunny day, walking at the back of the party along with a tall girl who, if my memory serves me right, would have been a few years older than me. We came up to a side road and Mary Poppins led her 'bonny little nips' around the corner, but the tall girl next to me suddenly dropped to the pavement like a stone. I suppose now that she had simply fainted, but what did little Mike Harmer do? Did he call the nurse? Did he run up and tug the nurse's sleeve? No, little Mike Harmer didn't bat an eyelid. He walked on as if nothing had happened, only speeding up his pace a bit to rejoin the main group, leaving the poor lass to fate. It was a while before the nurse realised that she had lost one of her flock.

To this day I don't know why I hadn't wanted to tell the nurse what had happened. Perhaps I was frightened or maybe I was just a dirty uncaring dog back when I was five years old. Who knows?

My lovely sister Maureen is two years older than me and as we were growing up in the Windy City on Spa Common, we were inseparable. I always thought Maureen to be more brother than sister. We had such good times together in those growing-up years.

I cannot ever remember it raining when we were young. Every

day was bright and sunny, and every day was a holiday. Maureen and I used help my mother on her wood round. There was a large old trolley which we loaded up with the logs that my father Edgie had cut up with his ancient saw bench and engine.

Mother would put our bay horse, Jack, into the trolley and away we went, mostly around Knapton and Paston, two small villages not far from the coast. Mother knew her customers well, so me and Maureen would carry the willow skeps of firewood to the customers' doors while Mother would spend time chatting to these folk. When the trolley was empty off we would head back towards home, though, often as not, Mother would pull up at a pub and have a glass or two of stout along with her Craven 'A' cigarettes, with me and Maureen being supplied with bags of crisps and drink.

Finally we would set off again, but not always straight home. We would frequently make a detour into Witton woods, a large wood outside North Walsham. What we then did was dependent on the time of year. During the summer and autumn mother would produce a handsaw and start to cut down dry timber. There would be no rest until the trolley was loaded. However, if it was winter or early spring mother would cut and tie up a trolley full of peasticks and linen props that she would hawk around North Walsham. So you see it was not always play. We would have to do some serious graft before we arrived home.

Once on the wood round on Knapton Street in Knapton, a small village near Mundesley, Mother had gone round to a small cottage. She called for us to bring a skep of wood, but she did not warn us what we were about to see. As we got to the open cottage door this little old lady came rushing out on her hands and knees. She had pads on her knees and mittens on her hands. Me and Maureen were shocked and ran back to the horse and trolley well frightened. The little old lady must have had some complaint as she could not walk and she crawled everywhere.

Maureen and I attended North Walsham Manor Road school and would usually come home for our lunch, but sometimes we would have to stay in school and have a school dinner which I hated. You see, I was not used to eating *Gorgio scran* (I had better explain that a *Gorgio* is a Romany word for a non-Romany - it used to mean someone who lives in a house - and *scran* is our word for food). The old teachers virtually forced you to eat it all up, whether you liked it or not. So I got a plan going. I had befriended two poor *chavies* (boys) who came from a children's home in North Walsham. These two had such a hunger about them that they would have eaten their grandmother if they had had one. Come lunchtime and the school's gruel was served; it reminded me of pig swill. My two new best mates needed no encouragement to help put away the food. In fact, they would have eaten the plate if it had been allowed. So you see, if you are fly enough there is always a way around life's problems.

Another time at school, I had a bit of a shock. I would then have been about 14 years old. Our form teacher, Mr Balls, asked my class to write a short essay on any subject. Even back then I did not mind doing a little writing, I quite enjoyed it. When I had finished the piece, I gave it the title 'On The Road To Norwich'. It was a simple idyllic thing, no more than a bit of nonsense. But Mr Balls had other ideas. On reading it he declared himself amazed and in his delight he awarded me three stars for my offering. He then took me to one side and said, "Harmer," (why don't these prats use your first name?), "I have tweaked that essay you wrote a little and entered it into the school's prize poem of the year competition". I protested, telling him that it couldn't be poetry because it didn't rhyme. "Harmer," he said "it's a free verse poem. It doesn't need to rhyme. I thought, "That's crap but do what you like".

Nothing happened for several weeks until one Friday afternoon the whole school, all five hundred and something pupils were gathered in the assembly hall. After a few speeches, the headmaster stood up and began to announce the result of the school's poetry prize. The words rang out: "In reverse order, third place goes to John Brown, second place to John Smith and it is my great pleasure to ask this year's winner to stand up and come collect the first prize, Michael Harmer!"

Readers, picture me with my knobbly knees and short trousers, having to stand up and, red-faced, accepting the deafening applause while thinking, "F**k this, I don't want to be poet laureate of the year. This is definitely not going to be doing anything for my street cred."

You see, readers, I would always tend to walk on the wrong side of the road and mix with the rougher and seedier elements in life's circles. This poem lark made me look a proper pansy. Believe me, I took a fair amount of ribbing over this. It was not my finest hour.

Just before I was about to leave school, a careers officer came to the school to sort vocations out for us pupils. My teacher told this officer that I had a way with words and maybe he should try and place me with a nearby printing work here in the town. What he did not know is that us Romanies are quite capable of finding our own work.

As soon as I left school I found a few part time jobs, and in the spring and summer I would go out to gather watercress and supply most of the shops in North Walsham. I would also work the local dumps, picking up metal and stuff to sell on, thus earning a tidy little living. You see if you were fly enough, and I was sure I was, then you could earn a living without signing up to the 9 to 5 brigade. After about a year, for some reason I took a job on a small farm. I thought I would work here just until I was old enough to get a driving license, and that's what I did. I left the farm in 1963 and I never worked for anyone regular ever again.

The Windy City

Where shall I start, you ask? I'll start where I always start my days. Down here on Spa Common, where once we lived in a railway carriage in the place we called 'The Windy City. Along the way I will try and find you a few more tales of the old boys I have met and had a few deals with.

I suppose I first got the taste for dealing at a young age, watching poor old Mum and Dad having a deal or two. When I was a youngster, Edgie, my father, would often go out and take me with him *monging* (begging) for old trees for firewood, which he would cut up and my mother, Mary Harmer, would *fence* (sell).

In those days Edgie had several old sheds on this bit of *puv* (field). We kept two old *grais* (horses), one to fetch the *cosh* (wood) in, and the other to take it out and *blue* (sell) it. There was also an old tin cartshed where Edgie kept an ancient stationary engine which drove the old saw bench. Hang on reader, I can feel a tale coming on already as I talk about the old saw bench. Living down at Mundesley was a bullock dealer by the name of Jack Watts. Jack's father was brother to old Smock Watts. He lived with old Sally Harmer, my dad's mother (Christ, I keep wandering off the plot – I think I might have writer's cramp...or is it rheumatism?). Back to Jack Watts – Jack called down here and asked Edgie if he could run some old oak sleepers down the centre of his saw bench to make them into posts. Edgie thought there might be a few *shants* (pints) in it and agreed to cut them for Jack.

Reader, let me put you in the picture – Edgie, as I said, had a very ancient 'Bamford' engine which ran a large cast iron saw bench. The engine was in the back of the shed in the yard. About five yards away was the saw bench. The bench was driven by a wide old webbing belt which had a few joins in it. Anyway, Edgie gets to work with a little help from my brother, Dick. On the bench goes the first oak sleeper. "Blast me," it made Edgie's old engine gasp. The oak sleeper was as hard as a rock. Halfway through, the long belt began to flap together. Somehow, the old belt (where it was joined) caught the other side of the belt and wrapped itself around the pulley wheel on the engine. It pulled the heavy old saw bench up into the air and through into the shed. It nearly *mullered* (killed) old Edgie and Dick. The belt was still flying around with the belt making a trench and throwing soil and stones out. Edgie could not get to the old engine to turn it off with all these missiles flying at them. In the end, Edgie and Dick could do nothing but leave it to run out of petrol. Jack Watts never did get his posts, but his sleepers nearly killed poor old Edgie.

Another thing I remember – my sister Maureen and I were coming into the yard one very dark night and to our amazement the yard was glowing. When we got over our fright, getting close to a pile of firewood, we saw that the bright light was coming from the wood. The wood was decaying elm, which I discovered gives off this luminous glow: how strange!

I had better tell you a little about living in a railway carriage. Edgie bought the *puv* down on Spa Common for £40 off a butcher in North Walsham. He then bought the railway carriage. He borrowed a horse drawn timber drug from a place he worked, a timber yard owned by Page. It was up the Norwich Road where the old canneries stood. He put the carriage on his *puv* and, as his family got larger, Edgie would make the railway carriage bigger by adding extra rooms. This carriage was larger than normal to start with as it had a guard's van on the back, thus making an extra bedroom.

There was no electric or water down at our place. We had to rely on paraffin lamps for light. For several years Edgie would get his water from our neighbour, Mr Simmonds, up at Orchard Farm. He would let us draw water from his well. This went on well until Mr Simmonds *mullered*. He was the old boy, if you remember in my last book, whose suit Edgie wanted! After the old *mush* (man) died, a relation of his took over and I don't think he was too pleased letting Edgie have his *pani* (water). So one day, just as Edgie arrived at the well, the mush lowered a dirty old pail which he had been feeding his *baulos* (pigs) with. It was covered with dirt. When Edgie got home he said to Mother, "that *sube-juk* (f*** dog) has been putting dirty pails down the well." Mother said, "it's his well...he can do what he likes. You will have to put the water on our place." Christ, Edgie was sick. It cost him £4.10s. Edgie was tight. When he had it put on, he did not have it near the railway carriage. Instead, we had a standpipe near the road, so Mother had to carry water a long way down at 'Windy City'.

We kept a fair amount of livestock: with the two *grais* (horses) we had pigs, goats, chickens, ducks and geese. We also had a fair few *juks* (dogs). That reminds me – I told you in my earlier book about old Tommy Manes from Mundesley. Tommy had an old *juk* he wanted to get rid of and he thought Edgie would like it. Well, one day when Mum and Dad were out – it was a Thursday, market day – Tommy left the *juk* with an older sister of mine, Jane. She decided to take a stroll and took the *juk* with her. It was not on a lead. About a mile away from us was a game farm owned by a Captain Barnard, Bacton Wood Mill Farm. The Captain had large flocks of Black Leghorn hens in large wire runs. Well, this old *juk* of Tommy Manes seemed to like the old *kanis* (chickens). It broke into the runs and went on a killing spree. My sister panicked and left it to it. When Edgie and Mary got home from the town, there was a *musker* (policeman) waiting for them. Edgie did not know anything about the *juk*, but the musker could see the *juk* in our yard. It had *mullered* loads of the Captain's *kanis*. Edgie got his *yogger* out and shot the *juk*. Edgie had three options: he would either have to pay the Captain a pound each for the *mullered kanis*, replace them with point of lay pullets, or go to court. Edgie bought the Captain more pullets even though the bloody *juk* did not belong to us!

When Mother and Father were *rommed* (married) they bought an old *vardo* (wagon) from an old *bokra engro* (shepherd) and went on the *drom* (road). They would buy up *shooshi* (rabbit skins), as well as *gunners* (sacks) and old bottles. All these items could be sold at *tatshops* (marine stores), so you could have a half tidy living. As the *chavies* (kids) came along they left the *tober* (road) and moved into the old railway carriage. There they dealt in firewood, peasticks and linen props which Mother would *hawk* (sell). Other times Mother would go into Norwich and buy china seconds from Looses in Magdalen Street. Also in Norwich she could buy saucepans, pans, lids, etc. to hawk around the countryside.

You see, years ago, old country folk could not get to Norwich and places, so they relied on people like my mother to sell them cheap china, kitchenware, etc. While Mother supplied the old *raklas* (women) with their wares, Edgie would buy *shooshi* and *kanis* (rabbits and chickens). He would dress them out and send them by train to Smithfield Market in London.

*

As well as the daily round of buying and selling, if they had time, they would turn out several gross of *tograms* (linen pegs), which always sold well. A good *togram* maker could make about 5 gross a day (that's about 720 *tograms*). To make *tograms* you need two things: a good peg knife, which must be razor sharp, and good hands. When you get older and when rheumatism sets into your *vasts* (hands), it becomes hard to grip the peg and the *churi* (knife). Peg making is a job which requires the peg maker to sit down and he must be comfortable. I tried a few years ago to teach an old friend of mine how to make pegs. It was impossible. It was scary to see him stick the bradawl into his *vast* when he was trying to make the holes. It's like many old trades; it's very hard for anyone to learn the skills.

Let me try and tell you, Reader, how to make *tograms*. You will find that the best wood for this is young straight willow. Other straight grained woodsuch as hazel wood are also good...they make for sturdy pegs, though it's much harder to mouth the pegs with hazel. Right, let's go *togram* making. After you have yourself some young straight willow you will first need to cut it. Bend the wood down fairly hard and use an upward cutting stroke with the *chiv* (knife) on the bend. As long as your *chiv* is sharp, it will slice through the wood as if it were butter. Cut off the sideshoots and trim the willow, leaving a stick no more than an inch thick. Next, peel off all the bark using your *churi* (knife), starting at the thickest end of the willow. When this is done the *costies* (sticks) must be stood up and allowed to dry. When they are nice and dry, use your *churi* in a scraping motion, starting again at the thickest end. Also trim and cut away any knots. You will then need a wooden block placed at a comfortable height to work on and a fairly heavy wooden club called a maul, as well as a piece of round wood about 1.5 inches in diameter with a piece cut out the length of your peg. I like my pegs to be 6 to 7 inches long. This piece of wood is your gauge to ensure all your *tograms* are of the same length. Then, using a fairly thick, sharp bladed knife, start to cut off your pegs, hitting them on the wood block with your moll.

The next stage is to get your tin for the pegs. To do this, you can cut up an old biscuit tin into half inch strips. You twist the tin around the stick and tap a small hole in each strip with a sharp awl. With your right hand put a small 'gimp' pin in the hole and tap it in with a very small hammer, then bend the remaining tin over the peg and hammer it flat. A deft twisting stroke with the peg will break the tin. Tap the edge down, and now you are ready to 'mouth' the peg. Great care is needed here, as you are dealing with a very sharp *chiv* (knife). On the bottom of the peg, opposite the nail, keep prising the blade into the peg until it

The author illustrates the art of togram manufacture:

1. Stripping the willow.
2. Chopping the wood with the maul.
3. Mouthing the peg.

parts, then hold the peg on your knee with your left hand and slip the *chiv* into the slot and pull the peg at a sharp angle. Do not push the *chiv*. Repeat this twice, leaving a nice shaped finish. Quickly shave each side to trim the finished peg. If you have read my instructions right you have made your first *togram*. If you think this is easy, good luck. You can't buy a good peg knife – you have to make one. Get yourself a good, thin, well worn kitchen knife and sharpen it up. You will also have to make the wooden handle, which needs to be longer than a normal handle. It's so you can hold it on your knee when you are making a *togram*.

Now, Reader, let's say you have made your first batch of pegs. You will now have to find a few *shobies* (shops) to sell them – *custi bok* (good luck)!

*

My mother had a brother whose name was Archie, but everyone called him 'Chinner'. In Romany it means to cut or chin the *cosh* (wood). Archie was a peg maker, and I doubt whether anyone in England made more pegs than Archie. He made them his entire life.

Archie lodged over near Grimston, Kings Lynn, with a nice old *Gorgio* (non-Romany woman). Archie got called up to serve for his country in the Great War. Off went Archie to sort out the German *koolis* (soldiers). When the war finally ended Archie did not return. The old *rakla* (woman) and others thought that Archie was *mullered*. So, in the village after the war a memorial stone was erected for the Poor Lost Souls, including Archie, whose name was carved on the stone. Apparently, however, Archie had thought he would have a walkabout like Paul Hogan in Crocodile Dundee. The poor old *rakla* nearly *mullered* when she was sitting in the *kair* (house) one day and in walked Archie. The old *bewer* (woman) thought he was a ghost! It seems as if

Chinner had opened the 'pearly gates' and walked out again!

My mother and I attended Archie's funeral at Grimston after he eventually did made his proper acquaintance with the grim reaper in the nineteen-seventies. I think my uncle, Bert Lamb, and his wife, Lily, had old Chinner's *togram* knife and tools. He was a funny old Romany.

Archie 'Chinner' Lamb's togram knives

Rust, Gunners & Tats

The last war made many Romany *mushes* very wealthy. Most of the Lamb family around North Walsham were a bit too old for the Army. My uncle Albert and Bert Lamb would collect *rust* (scrap) and metals from Red Cross depots which the British public had collected for the war effort. About three miles away is a small village called Dilham. The old *sky* (parson) got my Uncle Albert over to take away the rectory gates and iron railings to help the war effort. Albert collected them, then drove down to Dilham Hall to see a Scots farmer. Anyhow, the farmer took a shine to the gates and railings and bought them off Albert. They reappeared after the war on the front drive of Dilham Hall where they are still today! Everyone was a winner except the old *sky*.

I'll tell you another tale – that is, if you want to hear it – I'm sure you do.

Just before the war, my uncle Winks Lamb bought a heap of old *rust* off Mr Fulcher of Barton House Farm in North Walsham. The old *givengro* (farmer) was pleased he got a few *clods* (coins) for his *rust* off Winks. However, Winks was called up into the Army and duly served his time. After the war, Winks returned to Barton House Farm and asked the old *mush* if he had any *rust* to sell. Christ, the old *gilly* (man) went into a rage. He went mental – "Scrap," he shouted, "to sell you? What did you do with the last lot I sold you? You know what you done with it, you went and bloody sold it to Hitler and what did he do? He went and dropped it back in my field! No, I will never sell you any more as long as I live." It seems that during the war the Germans dropped a few small bombs in his field and he thought they were made from his scrap which he had sold Winks. He was a funny old *Gorgio* (non-Romany).

During the war and just after, some old Romanies were very

wealthy. If you had an old lorry or truck you could get a good living. You could sometimes pick a load of scrap up from old commons. People years ago would dump their rubbish on the local common. Many times I have picked up a truck load of *rust* from only two commons. When I first got started in this trade in about 1963, you did not have to go around and call for scrap. You could just ride around the local towns and villages and spot little heaps of it in folk's yards. At that time, changes were taking place: electricity was being put on to most village houses, so people were throwing out their old paraffin lamps, which were a good source of scrap. It was in the mid Sixties when the Americans started to buy up these old lamps, etc., and they started to be worth a good deal. You could get between £10 and £40 depending on how good it was. Also in the mid Sixties Americans began to buy old jug and bowl toilet sets, marble top washstands, etc. This opened up another dimension for anyone out on the *tober* (road) – knocking on *Gorgios'* doors. You could not go wrong, and everyone was earning.

Later on in this book, I will take you with me, Reader, as I go on the old knocker. That's if you want to come? Please yourself. But for the moment, let me tell you about the *chats* (things) out there. When I started out in 1963 I dealt mostly in old *rust*, *gunners* and *tats* - that's scrap, sacks and rags to you. The *tats* we would sell to old Archie King in Norwich. I think the Kings were a Jewish family. They were up at Ber Street. We would also sell him *smut* (brass) and other metals. He had a very *fly mush* (sharp man) working for him who would weigh your *covels* (things). His name was George Woods. He was one of the flyest mushes I ever came across. You would have to drop him some *loover* (money) or he would tuck you up on the scales. After you had tipped him, he would still try it on with you. So you see, Reader, you had to be on your toes with *Gorgios* like these around you. With old *tats* to earn good *loover* you had to pick out the *knits* (woollens) – these were worth a lot more *loover*. Handling old *tats* was a *hindity* (dirty) old job especially if they came from a *hindity kenner* (house). Sometimes they would have *joobs* (fleas) on them. Christ, talking about *joobs*, I am starting to itch. Let's change the subject.

> **Top Prices Paid . . . . . . Ready Cash**
>
> ## MRS. MARY HARMER
> ### Spa Common - North Walsham
>
> will call, in about ONE HOUR, and collect
>
> Any Old Rags, Woollen Wear, Old Iron, Lead, Brass, Copper, Pewter, Old Electric Coppers, Old Table Lamps, Old Carriage Lamps, Old Foot Scrappers, Brass Ornaments, Copper Kettles, Pewter Tea Pots, etc., Old Brass Fenders, Guns and Old Rifles, also Old Feather Beds and Old Car Batteries.
>
> Take care of this card for further use — **THANK YOU !**

One of the original cards used by the author and his mother

The best way to buy up old *tats* (rags) is to have some cards or bills printed. What you would do is have print a list on them of the sorts of *covels* (things) you wanted such as old rags, woollens, brass, copper, lead, old car batteries, scrap iron, etc. Also you would put your name and state that you would call back in one hours time to collect anything the house owner had found you. We would distribute around 100 bills around the houses at a time. Then you would find yourself a nice little *kitchema* (pub) and have a *jam jar* (glass) or two. Maybe sometimes you would buy something off of an old *Gorgio* in the *kitchema*. After about an hour you could start at the first *kenners* (houses) where you dropped your bills off. If you had a good day you would get maybe a truck load. Also if you saw any *rust* that you couldn't fit in, you would *pester* (pay) for it and return another time. Not a bad little life...you had just enjoyed a few *shants* (pints), hopefully you had bought a nice load of *tats*, etc., and got back home just after dinner time. You would then sort your *tats* out, taking out the *knits* (woollens), bagging them up, ready for the rag shop. Also you might have pulled out some tidy old clothes to *fence* (sell) on to poor old *Gorgios* who could not afford new clothes.

Old Tommy Manes from Mundesley had a sister called Mary Hawkins. She was a 'wardrobe dealer', meaning she dealt in secondhand clothes. She had a shop in North Walsham at the old butchery, which sadly has been demolished. Anyway, sometimes Mary would get us in to buy her old *tats* which she could not sell. We, at times, bought over a ton off her. At that time Mary was landlady at the Feathers Inn in North Walsham. She was always buying up gold, jewellery, etc. I think I am right in saying when she was a young *rakla* (woman) she would perform in circuses. She was a contortionist. Once, I was told, there was some major event on in North Walsham...the coronation or something. At the top of the town, near the Cross Keys Inn, Mary laid a narrow rug down to the town clock. She stood on the carpet, grasping the two corners, and in a flash rolled herself up in the carpet and rolled the full length of the market place, finishing up at the town clock.

Wrapped in a carpet, talking about old *tats*, can't we get on to a better subject? We were often called out to buy up any surplus rags after a jumble sale. This way you could get a fair amount of *tats*. Anyway, let's carry on. At a local village around here the old *Gorgios* sent for us to buy up the leftovers from a jumble sale in a church hall. A day or two later one of the villagers came to see us; it seems the old *sky* (parson) had hung his best Harris Tweed jacket up and it had disappeared. It contained his wallet with his *John Bradburys* in it, and also some personal bank cards, etc. They did not know if someone had bought his jacket or whether it had got in amongst the leftover *tats* we had bought. At the time we had a large quantity of old *tats* at our place and we had to empty all of them to try and find the old *sky's* jacket. We did not find it – someone must have bought it for two bob and found a nice bit of *loover* hidden away there. It's a lesson to you all: never take off your jacket at a jumble sale or someone will have it. It's a good job he did not take off his white collar, as they might have had another old *sky* walking about!

In Vicarage Street in North Walsham, before the street was demolished, there were rows of small houses and a few shops. One small shop was rented by Doreen Wright, Ray Wright's wife. Doreen mostly sold secondhand clothes, shoes and the like. One time, Doreen called us in to buy up some surplus old clothes which she was unable to sell. We drew up into the *shobi* (shop). It was very tiny, and the whole shop floor was covered with the biggest heap of *chokkers* (shoes) I had ever seen. Sitting on top of them was Doreen, laughing away. She was always roaring with laughter. It seems that in the shop there was a *rakla* (woman) who had found a nice red ladies' shoe but could not find the other one. Instead of putting all pairs of shoes back neatly, Doreen kept throwing them on this large pile. They never did find the missing red shoe.

By the way, Doreen's husband Ray had a fruit and vegetable round in the country where he would *hawk* his wares. In later years, Ray and Doreen opened up a bric-a-brac shop in the old Rising Sun Inn in North Walsham, one of the *kitchemas* where I used to *scimish* (drink). Ray and Doreen in later life also had a bric-a-brac down at Cromer, where they finished their years together. They were a lovely couple.

My Fair Lady & Other Folk

Let's now go back a few years. My dear sister Maureen and I, when we were very young (Christ, Mike! "Young" – you are now so old rumour has it you were seen swimming away from the Titanic!)...anyway, back to the tale. Maureen and I would be regular customers at the old Regal cinema in New Road. Sometimes if there was a certificate film showing you had to have an adult with you. Along with the other kids, we would stand outside the Regal, asking everyone who came to take us in. Most people would just walk past and ignore us, but if Doreen was coming she would take us in along with loads of other children. She was like Mary Poppins. She would sometimes fill an entire row of seats up with her gang of children. Maureen and I would go to the cinema most nights of the week. Our parents Edgie and Mary used to like a *scimish* (beer) so they would give us a handful of *loover* and to the Regal we would go. We would have plenty of ice-creams and drink, but going to the cinema every night came to haunt me years later! Let me tell you about it.

A few years ago a nice *monista* (woman) by the name of Kate lived over at Stalham. Kate and her husband would often come to my yard and buy bits and pieces. One day, Kate turned up in my yard. "Mike", she said,

"I'm putting on a musical production of My Fair Lady at Stalham High School and I need to borrow some props – can you help me out?"

"I will try," I said.

I would be on a loser – I wouldn't be taking any *loover* off the *mort* (woman). It's the story of my life. I have helped more lame dogs over stiles than Paul O'Grady. Maybe for all these good deeds there may be a place in heaven for me? I won't bet on it! Anyway, back to Kate. She needed a small iron stove and a copper kettle for a street urchin scene. I supplied them. As I was getting *nicksas* (nothing) for it, I was glad to see her *jell* (go). Before she went, she said,

"Mike, thanks very much for your help. I am going to give you something."

I thought to myself...it's starting to look a little better; she was a *custi rakla* (good looking woman) – maybe I will get a nice *choomer* (kiss) and a hug? Not my f*****g luck. Kate said,

"I am going to give you and your good wife two free tickets for My Fair Lady."

I couldn't believe this: musicals, I f*****g hate them! I would rather spend a week locked up in the *stirapen* (prison) up at Knox Road in Norwich. You see, Reader, as I told you, my sister and I went to the Regal cinema every night. The Regal being a small cinema, it was hard to get big major films down there, but if they showed the film for two weeks they could. My poor sister Maureen and I had to endure for a fortnight the musical Call Me Madam, which had done our *sheros* (heads) in. So, Reader, let's just say I did not want to see a musical again.

*

Talking about musicals – when he had a few *shants* inside of him, Edgie would sometimes spontaneously perform a song or two in the local *kitchemas*. One day in the White Swan in North Walsham, Edgie, as always, was getting a little on the *motty* (drunk) side, so the old boys in the White Swan were kidding him to give a rendering of the old music hall song 'The Old Grey Coat'. To the delight of the whole crowd, Edgie got into his stride and started to sing and as he sang he kept pulling the old landlord's coat to add emphasis to the words of the song: '*If the old grey coat keeps another year afloat it will take the old age pension*'. Christ, the old *mush* went mental and shouted at him to leave. Believe it or not, Edgie got a red card and had to leave the pub. He had to finish 'The Old Grey Coat' out in Church Street. The landlord. Sid Sexton, was a member of the Salvation Army would you believe it, and he did not drink and was a proper old *juk* (dog). Some of the old boys could not take a joke.

I remember another time when Edgie was put out of a *kitchema*. It was in the summertime at The Lighthouse pub in Walcott when we had some relations staying over for their holidays. One Saturday night, they all decided to go on a pub crawl down by the coast to have a few *sherberts* (beers). As there were a fair few of them, they went in three cars – Edgie went with my mother's brother, Hobby Lamb. You must remember Hobby from my first book? He was the one who threw Edgie's *holofers* (socks) in the p**s pot! Everything was going well when Edgie and Hobby drew up to The Lighthouse and started to *scimish* (drink). Edgie didn't pace himself and got a little too much down his neck and started to get well *motty*. He then started to let out a few Anglo-Saxon words and got a red card. Edgie was off out of the *kitchema*. Not long afterwards, along came the other pub crawlers. Mother, on seeing Edgie standing outside, said, "What are you doing standing outside the *kitchema*?"

Edgie replied, "The old landlord has f*****g thrown me out!"

So my mother said, "Where's Hobby?"

Edgie replied, "That *minge* is still in the pub playing cards."

Hobby left his old brother-in-law standing outside – what a mate to have! Yes, Edgie got a red card and was sent off the pitch, plus a match ban.

I had my first *shant* in the Lord Nelson Inn in North Walsham.

It had what is known as a 'snug', which is a small room out of sight of the main bar – a place where you could be private. At that time the landlady was Mrs Grimes, who would let young underage drinkers taste the sweet delights of their first drink. I was very much like Edgie, in that I could down several *shants*, but I would soon get *motty*. Unlike Edgie, I would never swear or make myself a nuisance. I would want to treat the whole *kitchema* to a drink. Sometimes the next morning I would wake up and feel in my *putsi* (pocket) for my *loover* and think I had been robbed. My old *putsi* was bare, like Old Mother Hubbard's cupboard! The night before I'd have treated half of North Walsham to a *scimish* (drink). I then had to get up the *tober* and earn some more *loover*. Funny old world: if you don't watch out, that old amber nectar will rule you.

Another time, I remember I was over at the Red Lion in Aldborough just before the fair, which falls on 21 June; I had some good sessions in that old *kitchema*. On this occasion I was drinking with a good crowd of old Norfolk boys, and we shifted some *scimish*. This was pre-breathalyser days, when if you could jump into your old *jam-jar* (car), you could drive it. At the end of the night we were saying our farewells as *motty mush* do. We were having a laugh, and someone was p***ing up beside my old truck wheel, when I spotted that I had a flat tyre and no jack. I got the old spare wheel down, which was fixed to the roof of the old truck. Because it was an old Austin 10 Army Truck, it was a bit of *kinder* (shit) but old Mike Harmer never did have anything too flash. Even now, I still drive old trucks. I have seen newer things on Antiques Roadshow than the one I have now.

Right, I thought: what can I do? It's getting late and no jack! Old matey is still p*****g up my wheel…he must have a tank on him like a fire engine. Anyway, he has just finished and is packing it away! I think, let me get all these *motty* old boys to lift my truck, and then I won't need a jack! So I *moody* (kid) them up and I say "I bet you can't lift that old truck up!" That got the lads going. There were enough of them to bloody carry that old truck to Alby Horseshoes and back. I started to undo the wheel nuts, and then every *motty mush* wanted to help. One started to undo a nut, and another grabbed the wheel brace off him and it developed into a fight. Two of them started *cooring* (fighting), and the *claret* (blood) started to fly. I somehow managed to calm things down. The two pugilists shook *vasts* and all was well. Then I had about a dozen old *motty* boys lifting my old truck up, while I tried to put the wheel on. In all this mayhem, I could find only one wheel nut. I banged that on as tightly as I could, bade them farewell, and left the drinking band there, still outside the old Red Lion. I somehow managed to get home with one nut!

An earlier generation of the Kidd family

Here's another little tale for you concerning the same old truck. I took my mother to Aldborough fair. Luckily, Mother had gotten a fair few stouts into her. She and I were drinking in the Red Lion, and I can remember most of the good old Romanies who were there that night! Russell Gray, Stanley Gray and Felix Gray – cousins of mine – had their families with them. I also remember little Titch Pope from South Creake was there, as well as several Lambs and their families, who were all related to me. Also there were Sidney and Nigger Kidd and their sons Mike, Arthur and Dougie. They had a float full of horses all tied up on the green. Richard Davies, the Cromer lifeboat coxswain and fisherman, was doing a nice bit of step dancing. It was a good night, and we were doing what all Romanies do, meeting up and having a few laughs and yarns and getting well and truly *motty*.

Anyway, every good thing must come to an end, and it was time for us to say goodbye. I put mother into the front of the old truck and we were about to leave the *wellgorus* (fair) when a chap I knew from North Walsham, Jack Russell, appeared. He was a little on the short side, and he was no Brad Pitt, but he could pick up young *rawnees* (girls). At the fair that night was his next conquest. She was a little mousey type who lived in North Walsham. She had biked over to the fair and was looking for romance. Christ, she certainly found that with Jack. He asked me if I could take him and his date home. My mother, who would always 'help a lame dog over a stile', said "jump in the back of the truck and we will take you home." Jack threw the young *rawnee's* bike in the truck, they climbed in, and we were off on the 12 miles to North Walsham.

I knew what Jack was like; he would make love to an eel if he could hold it! Mother luckily was starting to doze off in the old truck. About two miles along the road I glanced at the inside truck mirror, because we were going down a dark wooded road. The back of the truck was well lit up, and I could not believe my old *yoks* (eyes)! Jack had gotten the *togs* (clothes) off the young *rakla* and he was at it like an Easter bunny rabbit! The young *rakla* didn't look like she was complaining, either. My God, if my Mother had turned her head around, she would have gone mental. At last we reached the old town, and I got out and lifted up the tilt and undid the tailboard. There were Romeo and Juliet, who had just managed to put their *covels* (things) back on, and the back of the old truck was still steaming. Talk about a passion wagon – there's some funny old boys about. The length they will go to for a little bit of nookie.

*

I think I told you in my last book about me and Cliffy Cushions. He's my old mate who still runs a scrap yard here in North Walsham. We wrote off an old boy's *jam-jar* when we were *motty*, driving home from Great Yarmouth. At the time of this tale I was driving an old 1938 Vauxhall car. It was a right old heap of *kinder* (shit). Several years ago on a Saturday night, Cliffy Cushion, Hank Platton from Sheringham, his cousin Tec Platton and I all piled into my old jam-jar and went to a dance at the Red Lion in Aylsham. This was a fairly lively old *kitchema*, as it had a dance hall up a flight of stairs in the pub yard. We started putting back a fair number of bottles of *sherbert* (beer) and at closing time we bought a crate of *scimish* (beer) for the journey home. I then had to take Hank and Tec back to their home in Sheringham.

We were drinking the bottles as we were driving and throwing the empties at walls, etc., as we went. I don't know what happened but I got a little close to the side of Ingworth bridge, and we heard a bit of a bang but carried on to Sheringham. By the time we got there it was into Sunday morning and I was nearly out of petrol. When we got to Beeston Common, Hank woke up an old garage *mush* named Prince. He opened up his pumps and topped us up. Next we dropped Hank and Tec at Common Lane. It was now about 1 o'clock in the morning. Outside Hank's *kair* (house) was an old Fordson Major tractor, which he used for his wood business. He insisted on starting it up, because he wanted to show what a good tractor it was. My God, it was early morning – he woke most of Sheringham up! The noise was unbearable, and the whole road of folk were opening their windows, shouting at Hank to turn the tractor off. Hank was swearing at them, and Cliffy and I decided to leave this mad melee before the *gavvers* (police) came and *stiffed* (arrested) us. The next morning when I awoke and looked at my old car, it was a wreck. I had taken out the entire side of it! My *jam-jar* was a total write off. Were you to repeat this little episode today, they would lock you up in the *stirapen* (prison) for six months.

*

Another incident that took place was several years ago, when Edgie and my mother, Mary, were taken over to Briston by Sidney and Nigger Kidd to look at a *grai* (horse) which Edgie was looking to *kin* (buy). I don't recall if they bought it, but it seems once they got over there, Sidney and his brothers–Mike, Spencer, Bert and Gimlet Kidd...all lovely old Romany *chals* (boys)–did not want Edgie and Mary to leave. So the whole clan went on the *scimish* for three whole days. On the third day the *motty* bunch got to Coltishall and were betting one another £5 a time who could back their *jam-jars* nearest to the river edge without the car falling in. After that they all decided to go for a swim. The men stripped off their *togs*, tied their silk *dikloes* (scarves) around their private parts and jumped into the River Bure. When the *dikloes* got wet they fell off and they were all soon *nongo* (naked). It was in the height of summer and this caused mayhem with the posh holidaymakers. I think someone called the *muskers* (police) and they all nearly got *stiffed* (arrested).

When, finally, the merry band got a little nearer to North Walsham, Edgie and Mary walked home. Some said that those old Romany *chals* would *scimish* until the *groovnis* (cows) came home. They lived on the old amber nectar. I don't think Edgie and Mary bought the *grai* (horse) off of Sidney Kidd. After all that scimishing they must have been *kak-looverd* (penniless).

In November 1963 poor old Edgie was on his last lap. He was in Cromer Hospital because he had just had a stroke. Sadly, a week later he passed away. Anyway, his old mate Sidney Kidd from Briston and his wife Nigger heard that poor old Edgie was getting ready to meet the Grim Reaper and decided to visit him in the *naflinken* (hospital). I think they were a little bit on the *motty* side. In they go looking for poor old Edgie, Sidney clutching a large bottle of whiskey. It was not long before they were shown the door. Their hearts were in the right place, but for Edgie his drinking days were at an end. God bless him. Most old Romany *chals* that I have known are very drink orientated. It seems as soon as a *kitchema* door is open, they are there.

*

I, myself, believe that most if not all Romanies are very social in their behaviour and have this need to get together within the framework of fellow Romanies. They seem to hate loneliness and they thrive on company. I think the drinking is a habit acquired to strengthen their family ties. If you come upon a group of Romanies – and by this I mean real true Romanies, not *posh-rats* (half-bloods) or *flat-mushes* (*Gorgios* pretending to be Romanies) – you might think as you meet them in groups that they are very boastful and loud people, but if you take the trouble to get to know them, you will find a very rare species of mankind. You will be amazed at their understanding and willingness to share their secrets and ambitions with you. A nicer bunch of humans you will struggle to find. Let's face it, you will be conversing with Orientals who over a thousand years ago graced the land of the Punjab in Northern India. Is that not a feat of human interaction?

Reader, where do I take you now? What I am trying to impress upon you are the merits of the almost extinct Romany race. Heaven forbid if we ever lose them completely: they are now part and parcel of old Great Britain, the same as the red K6 telephone kiosk or the red Routemaster bus. The Romanies are becoming just as rare. You must search them out, delving into dark corners and secluded dingles.

Do you remember Mumper's Dingle in George Borrow's Romany *Rye*? Where old Mrs Herne *drapped* (poisoned) him? You see, Reader, in the 19th Century old Mrs Herne did not want *Gorgios* to learn the Romany ways and customs, but all that is past us. Now you must still search out these ingenious people. It's like searching for the abominable snowman. We now all live in a multi-cultural society and I think we are beginning to learn to abide and live with people of different cultures. It's a measure of man's progress, when some time in the future all races will be equal.

Over time Romanies have mixed or interbred with others and the *ratti* (blood) has been somewhat diluted. To find a pure Romany these days is as difficult as finding a *minditsi* (virgin) in Holloway *stir* (prison). That's why, in the past, Romanies were afraid to let *Gorgios* into their world. You see, Reader, in the past on the *drom* (road) were other elements of society – tinkers, footpads, *cushni mengros* (basket makers) and *turnpike sailors* (tramps), all very allied to Romanies, but completely different. Some of this rabble started to *romm* (marry) into Romany clans. I, myself, think this was the start of the decline in the true *ratti* of the Romany. We have had vast numbers of Romanies settling down and moving into *bricks* (houses), and the *chavies* (children) have started to attend school and become educated. All these factors in turn have thinned down the Romany blood.

Today, we are left with a very depleted race of Romanies, who remain very proud of their heritage and upbringing. A finer and prouder people you will be pushed to find. I suppose it's down to guys like myself to remember and try and instill into you the old ways and tales of these very fine and noble people. Long may they survive. It took them over a thousand years to reach these shores and it would be a shame and a very sad loss to let them vanish completely – so I say to you, Reader, search them out and *rokker* (talk) to them. They're like a corner shop – you only miss it when it's no longer there. In this very nice, small country of ours, I feel there is room here for all of us. Respect your fellow man and you will be a greater man yourself.

Christ, I am glad I got that off my chest! I never knew I had it in me! Right, my lovely Reader, you must now be getting a little bored, with me running on. You bought this book, I think, to hear nice old tales, so let's find you a few more, if I can. Here we go! This old writing is harder than making ten gross of *tograms*.

Albert Lamb & Other Good People

Only last year a very dear cousin of mine, Albert Lamb, sadly passed away. I think he had a good life – I am sure he did. Tears still come to my *yoks* when I try and remember him, a lovely Romany *chal*. He has left two lovely daughters, both *custi raklas* (good women). Albert, in his time, like any true Romany chal, did most of his buying and selling at the *stigurs* (doors) of old *Gorgios*. Albert *rommed* (married) Queenie Wilson, from a well known Romany family. Anyhow, Albert went up the *tober* to get a little *loover* together to support his family.

Old Wilson and his *mort* (wife), Queenie's mum and dad, would watch Albert go out each day but he seldom brought anything home! So, after a while, old Wilson said to Queenie, "I don't think that *mush* of yours is going to be much good for you."

"Why not?" asked Queenie.

"Well," old Wilson said, "he goes out but don't seem as if he is buying anything."

What poor old Wilson did not know was when Albert went out buying each day up the *tober*, he would always, if he could, *blue* (sell) the *covels* he had bought on the way home. Maybe if he had bought antiques he would sell to an antiques shop. If he had bought *tom-foolery* (jewellery), he would call in at a jewellers, or if it was scrap or metal he would sell to a marine store dealer. You see, old Wilson did not know half the story. Albert always had an empty van or car, for he had *blued* all his covels before coming home.

Another time, my two sons and I were demolishing a large old malting building in Dereham when along came Albert to tell us a few nice old yarns. We liked to hear them. He started up by

Albert Lamb as a lad back in the 1930s

saying mysteriously, "I got off."

"Got off what, Albert?" I asked.

"I didn't have any lights on my bike, and the *musker* (policeman) stopped me!"

"And then what happened?" We had to coax it out of him.

"Well," he said, "they fined me £2."

"You got off light." I said, "When was that? Recently?"

"No," he said, "back during the war!"

Christ, we could not stop laughing. Albert was going back fifty years – what a gas!

Years before this when we were still living in the old railway carriage, Albert would drop by and to get a start on a Monday morning we would let him have a fair few old heavy corn sacks. Albert would put a bit of *pani* (water) on them to make them heavy, then wrap them up along with some old coats and *tats* and stuff some gunners (sacks) inside them, thus making them look like sacks or rags. He was not long in getting a half tonne together then off he went to Archie King, the marine store dealer in Ber Street in Norwich to sell his wet sacks for rags. These old marine dealers would tuck you up if they got half a chance, but some old *fly* boys like Albert, would tuck them up. Also, don't take this as the gospel truth, but I think Albert's dad (my mother's brother)...his name was Albert too...was once driving over Potter Heigham river bridge when he nipped an old boy up against the bridge wall. I don't know if he *mullered* him or just injured him, but Albert got put away in *stirapen* (prison) for six months. After that the council installed a set of traffic lights on the bridge, which are still there today.

My cousin Albert had a sister whose name was Molly Lamb. She lived in Norwich and would come by train to North Walsham and borrow my Mother's old bike and go around villages out here, *calling* (selling) her wares. I think she mostly sold women's *covels* (things). She still has a daughter, Caroline, who lives in Norwich. I last saw Caroline at Albert's funeral. Albert lived at Shipden with his daughter, Sally. She's a nice *rakla*, and she always sends me a card at Christmas and Easter, bless her. Albert has a brother, Maurice. He used to run a haulage business in Horncastle, but he is retired now.

Albert Lamb with his mother, Ginny Lamb - September 1963

Unfortunately, the only time we meet up is at funerals. I think a lot of the old Romany families don't get together enough. They have so much to give to each other, old tales and reminiscing. It seems as if they have stopped being like true Romanies who spent most of their time meeting up, socialising and years ago the only way to spread news was to pass it verbally. It's all getting so sad; Romanies, like *Gorgios*, are coming into the modern world of high technology, relying on mobile phones and iPads.

Believe it or not, I myself have been introduced to the iPad. I find it interesting, but very time consuming and I have yet to understand its full merits. I had to adapt to an iPad in order to sell my last book on Amazon and other internet sites. So I was forced, against my better judgement, into using one.

Reader, turn that mobile phone and iPad off and let us, once again, try and find some more old characters. I will see if we can find them, but I tell you it's getting harder. Every time one of them *mullers* there is not another one to take his place.

Romanies of today do not act in the same old ways. They seldom dress in the old manner and sometimes when I meet a *needi* (traveller) and throw a few Romany words at him, he is surprised and perplexed and sometimes ashamed to be a Romany. How awful is that? Never be ashamed of who you are. Always be proud – stand tall and dismiss those who dismiss you! We as Romanies have survived the stigmas and sometimes the horrors and persecution that we have had to endure for over a thousand years. We are who we are, a proud and noble race, and long may we continue.

I am very glad that in my time I have witnessed some truly wonderful Romany people. Most, sadly, have now gone. Let's not forget them and, Readers, if any of you have the tiniest drop of Romany *ratti* (blood) in your veins, stand up and remember who you are. Try your hardest to honour our memories and inspire into your siblings the meaning of the Romany trail, which ran all the way from India to these beautiful shores. George Borrow, in the 19th Century, was of the opinion that the Romany race would die out. How wrong was he? We are now in the 21st Century and we are still here and so we should endeavour to keep the spirit of the race alive for the future.

*

Back to the present. Reader, let me tell you about two nice old Romanies from Attleborough who passed away many years ago now. They were old Tommy and Amelia Gray. What a fine couple of true Romanies. They were once interviewed by the Eastern Daily Press. There was a lovely photo of them: Amelia had that lovely lived-in face that most Romany *raklas* have. Her lovely old *mui* (face) was full of deep creases and wrinkles acquired by living a Romany life beside smoking *yogs* (fires) over the years. I could say she had more lines on her face than a geological map of the Himalayas. But let's put this joking to one side and carry on with the tale. The journalist asked old Amelia and Tommy a few questions and photographed them leaning on a *stigur* (gate) outside their *kair* (house). Old Tommy told him how he used to tend to the *grais* (horses) when he and Amelia were *hatching* (stopping) on commons and how he minded the *vardo* (wagon). Then the journalist turned to Amelia and asked her how she met Tommy. She thought for a moment, then she replied, "I must have met him first thing in the morning before my *yoks* (eyes) were open." What a one liner! Such lovely dry humour, typical of the Romanies.

In the 1950s my mother's mother, Mary-Ann Lamb, was living with us, as she was getting *puro* (old) and she could not look after herself. Remember what I told you about Romanies. They all looked after their loved ones to the very end. She had been living in an old *vardo* on her *puv* (field) at Catch-Pit Lane in North Walsham and her health was failing. My mother decided that she should come to our place and stay and we would care for her in her last days. The old woman was still very strong minded and stubborn. Any how, one market day – that would have been on a Thursday – my sister Maureen and I had to look after her. Easier said than done. Since it was a Thursday, my mother and father were up in town on the old *sherbert*. We were under strict orders not to let Granny out! I expected the old dear started to get a bit of a thirst on and she started to put on her *togs* and her *chokkers* (boots) while Maureen and I tried to restrain her. But the old Romany *mort* (woman) was not having any of this. She was adamant that nothing would stop her. So there we were, walking up the *tober* with a frail eighty-seven year old heading for the *ginger beer shop* (pub). It was a good mile up to the town. I seem to remember that when we arrived my mother went mental. The old granny demanded some *scimish* and Mother tried to calm her down. When they got her a *half-shant*, she calmed down. Mother then had to get her a taxi home.

As I said before in this book, to Romanies, drinking was the core of their life. Granny's *rom* (husband) had had their old *vardo* made by Leonards of Soham in Cambridgeshire. Old Mary-Ann lived in the wagon with my uncle, Winks Lamb. The old gal would walk down to the town and go into the first pub, which was the Rising Sun, which was kept by Lou Lancaster. She would order a stout and pay for it with a gold sovereign. Old Lou took several off Mary-Ann; at that time, they were worth about twenty-five shillings each. He was a cunning old *juk*.

Most of the daughters of Butty Lamb (my father's mother) got *rommed* (married) to *flat mushes* (non-Romanies). When my mother *rommed* Edgie, he had a little Romany *ratti* in him. My aunt Milly *rommed* Billy Hudson, 'Tater Billy', who was a *mumper* (half-blood). My aunt Daisy Lamb *rommed* George Adams, a *Gorgio*. Ada Lamb, my mother's oldest sister, married Charlie Gray, a Romany *chal* (boy). They had a daughter, Ruby, who I think *rommed* a Pope from South Creake near Fakenham. There are still a few Popes over there. Gilly, Russell, Felix, Stanley, Harry and Charlie Gray were all Ada Gray's children. Charlie – who had the nickname 'Dummy' because, unfortunately, he was born deaf – was very noisy and agitated. He lived with his mother at Sloley near Worstead. My mother had an older brother, Bob Lamb, who lived down in Essex. Bob had a son who was deaf and dumb but he was altogether different, as he was very quiet. As you can see, Reader, when a Romany comes off the *tober* and settles down, he starts to lose his true identity. He also loses his

Romany appeal and he starts to get very boring, like a *Gorgio*. When you capture and tame a wild animal or bird, you take its vitality of life away and reduce it to a shell of its former self. Romanies, like wild creatures, express themselves better when they are free and unfettered.

*

My mother's sister Ada lived over at Sloley. Edgie, my father, once *blued* (sold) Ada's son Harry Gray a half tidy old *tit* (female horse). Harry only lived about four miles away at Sloley near Worstead. Edgie and Harry slapped one another's *vasts* (hands), Romany style, and sealed the deal in the traditional manner. Harry drove the old *tit* home and he was pleased with what he had bought.

It was a warm summer's eve and that *rarde* (night) Edgie laid his *shero* (head) down on his feather pillow in the old railway carriage with the *glazer* (window) open. he soon drifted away into a sound sleep. Then, in the middle of the night as Edgie lay next to the open window, he was awakened by hot breath blowing over his face. Edgie was a little *thrashed* (frightened), until he realised that looking through the window was the old *grai* (horse) he had just that day sold to Harry Gray. It did not want to leave old Edgie. Harry kept taking it back to Sloley but it would keep returning. In the end, Edgie gave Harry a little *loover* back and kept the old *tit*.

By the way, did I say, the name of Edgie's railway carriage was apt, named 'The Windy City'. It was always windy down there with the coming and going of everyone on the *tober*. It still is. I live on the same site and there are always people passing through. If only it could talk.

The Dealing Life

I told you Readers in the last book that l left school in 1957. I did not work anywhere regular until after about a year, when I went to work on a farm with Cyril Bell. He was one of old Cockle Bell's boys. The farm was at Colby, near Aylsham. The old *givengro* (farmer) was a Mr Hicks. These people were very strict religious folk and they were a little on the tight side. They would pick a farthing out of a cow's turd! It was an eight to five job that did not appeal to me too much. I would be working in them old *puvs* (fields) and would see the old dealing boys driving by in their lorries and vans and somehow I got the bug. I did not like staying in the same place too long. I stuck it out for about three years. Then I passed my driving test, bought myself an old army truck, told the old *gilly* (man) what to do with his job and I was off up the old *tober*. I was like a wild animal just let out of its cage. I started to put myself about a bit – I think it was about 1960, the start of the 'swinging sixties'. All those young *bewers* (girls) in those *custi* (good) little mini skirts...cor, I better cool down...I am starting to get all hyped up. It won't do my old ticker a lot of good. Cool down, Mike, you old fool. Right, Reader, here we are: the 'swinging sixties', little old Mike in his old green army truck...let's have fun. Let's get up that old *drom* (road) and start to earn some good *loover*.

I can remember one of the first deals I ever had, which happened over at Barton Turf. An old *mush* owned a small garage called Mill Garage, which is still there to this day. Behind the garage were the remains of a very old mill – it's still there. Anyway, the old *mush* kept all his old scrap car batteries in the mill. He was an old narky *mush*, hard to get on with. He himself was not too fond of other people. He was nicknamed 'Bent Axle', a funny nickname. I don't know why, but old Bent Axle took to me and seemed to like me. Perhaps it was my charm? I don't think so! He took me and showed me all the old batteries in the old Mill.

I have never seen so many. Back in the day you could get good *loover* for them. I soon had a deal with Bent Axle. Blast, he had some batteries: I piled them up on my old army truck and I had a job to drive the eight miles home.

The next day I was up with the lark. I put a drop of petrol into the old truck (it was 32p a gallon then) and drove up the *tober* to Kings of Norwich with my load. Just outside North Walsham, near Westwick Hall, I got a puncture and pulled over next to Westwick Park entrance. I decided to pull into the park to sort it out and change the wheel. Would you believe it, pulling in on the rough ground I heard an almighty loud bang and a crash. I got out and looked. Christ, the old army truck's springs had broken and both they and the wheels had come through the floor of my truck! I had to get a breakdown truck out from a local garage. He took one look at it and said, "You must be mad; you must have a tonne and a half on this poor little truck." I was still learning – the bloody hard way, I would think!

I had to get myself a bigger truck. I knew two old *chals* who had a little *tat* shop in Mariner's Lane in Norwich. It was a tiny yard near King Street, like in Steptoe and Son. I told them what happened to my old truck and that I had to borrow a truck until I bought another. These were a couple of nice old boys. One of them was Tommy Knowles. He only had one *herri* (leg). His partner was Bob Cousens. It was said that Tommy Knowles and his brother both lost a leg on the very last day of the war. How about that for a bit of bad luck?

Back to Steptoe's. I asked the two old marine store dealers if they knew of a small lorry that might suit me. I think Bob Cousens was the first one to reply. He said, "I know just the thing for you! It won't be too much *loover*."

"Where is it Bob?" I asked.

"It stands outside the Larkman pub." Cor, that was a rough old area, rougher than the Bronx in New York. Bob said, "Call in at the boozer and ask the landlord. The *mush* it belongs to sometimes lodges in the pub and sometimes he lives outside in the old lorry cab." What a funny old world! I drew over to the *kitchema* and went inside, half expecting to see Clint Eastwood, The Man with No Name, sitting in the corner, drinking whisky with his poncho on!

It was very dark and gloomy inside, more like the Black Hole of Calcutta. It was one of those pubs where you wiped your feet on the way out. Luck was on my side, for the *gilly* who owned the *moulder* (lorry) was inside. He looked like he would mug you for two bob. I *pestered* (paid) for a drink for him and myself, but I never bought 'Clint' a drink – he had a bottle of whisky and he did not look in the mood for conversation. The *mush* and I *jelled* (went) outside. It was a clean little lot and the *mush* was not too flush so I bought it. It was a nice tidy Bedford Type B, the sort *needis* (travellers) liked. We slapped hands and binded the deal. I was quite pleased and was about to drive it off when the mush shouted at me, "Hang on mate!"

I said, "What's up?"

"What's up?" he said, "My bloody milk is in the lorry."

It seems that as he sometimes lived in the lorry, the milkman used to drop him milk off in the lorry. Well, now he had his *loover* for the lorry and he had his *tud* (milk), and I had a nice little Type B Bedford to get up that *tober* and earn *a bitti loover* (a little money). Only this time I must not overload it like I did with old Bent Axle's batteries, bless him. Every time I wanted an old *moulder* I would go and see Tommy Knowles and Bob Cousens. They put me on to several more lorries over time. Every one was a good one – but, Reader, why was Clint Eastwood in the Larkman pub? Perhaps he was after A Fistful of Dollars.

Talking about vehicles, I once took my brother-in-law, Peter Purdy, to buy a Dodge van off Jack Leveridge from Cromer. Jack was a fly old Romany *chal*. The old van was not too special; in fact it looked like a bit of *kinder* (shit). Anyhow, Peter bought it and *pestered* (paid) him. He then said, "Pull up at Roughton Garage and I will put a drop of petrol in – it's nearly out of fuel." Off we went. Peter pulled up at the garage and was starting to fill it when he stopped. I said, "What's up, Peter?"

"I don't know," he said, "the petrol is running out." He squatted down and peered under the van. "Bloody hell!" he cried.

I asked, "What's up?"

"What's up?" he replied, "the old van has not got a petrol tank on it."

"It must have," I said, "...it can't run on nothing."

Peter opened the van's doors and looked inside, and – would you believe it – behind the driver's seat was a one gallon petrol can. Did I laugh! Peter did not! What a stunt to pull! You would not have gotten too far up the *drom* with only a gallon of fuel in a can. These old boys are sharp out there. Remember, buyer, beware! Do not part with your *loover* too quickly, because a fool and his money are soon parted.

Aunt Milly Hudson and Tater Billy

In my last book I told you about old Aunt Milly Hudson and Tater Billy from Holt. 'Course I told you: now pay attention and remember or we will be here all night. Milly and Tater – Christ, they were a rum couple. Those two would get wrong with the stones in the road. Tater Billy bought a large old motor bike, complete with a sidecar. He would sometimes use this when he was sharpening old lawn mowers and tools for old *Gorgios* (non-Romanies). He would put old Milly in the sidecar. Old Milly was a bit of a lump, so that used to put the pressure on the old sidecar!

One hot Sunday afternoon in the middle of summer – it was a scorcher – Milly and Tater Billy came out our way and here, on the common, they bought an old kite wagon off of old Rubber Burton, who had a *puv* down here near us. Where did they get all these nicknames from? 'Rubber Burton' – haha! Anyway, Milly and Tater Billy had a deal and bought the old *vardo* (wagon) off Rubber. Because it was only just up the road from our railway carriage, they pulled the old motorbike up outside and Milly got out of the sidecar and she and Tater Billy came to see us.

Edgie and I had been out across an old field opposite our place doing a bit of poaching or something – I can't remember now – but it was a sweltering Sunday afternoon and Edgie and I were hot, hungry and thirsty. We were about to climb over the old hedge and come into our yard when Edgie spotted Tater Billy's motor bike. Edgie said, "Don't go in yet. Let's lay under these old trees until they are gone." Edgie was never too keen on Milly or Tater Billy, so we lay and wait. We were being bitten alive by flies, we were hungry and parched, and still the motorbike and sidecar were there. At last, we couldn't wait any longer and we had to draw in. When we entered the carriage old Milly said, "I am glad you came, old brother-in-law; we did not want to leave until we saw you!" We were shattered, and it was hours before they left for Holt. What a strange couple – once they were in your *kair* (house), you could not get rid of them. It was like trying to get rid of the measles.

Another time down at Holt, Milly and Tater Billy were at home. They had two old wagons: one they lived in and they *soved* (slept) in the other. These two old *vardoes* were their pride and joy. Tater Billy was always washing them down and giving them a polish. However, one day along came Milly's sister Daisy from East Dereham. She was as crazy as Milly, or nearly! Daisy brought with her an old *bokra mush* (shepherd). Tater and Milly weren't pleased. Daisy and the old *mush* were well *motty* . Daisy had the old mush's *loover* tied up in her silk *diklo* (scarf). Milly and Tater Billy put up with them for a time until the old *bokra mush* unzipped and started pissing up Tater Billy's old *vardo's* wheel. Strewth, Tater went mental and put them a-going. Never was he so insulted in his life. It took Tater ages to scrub the old *bowler* (wheel). Next time we saw Tater he said to my mother, "Mary, your *divvy* sister brought that dirty old *mush*. What do you think he did, Mary?"

She replied, "I don't know!"

"Don't know?" Tater said, "That dirty old *mush* pissed all over my wagon wheel, that dirty old *juk*."

Every time we saw Tater Billy he hadn't forgotten it. Daisy was alright; she had the old *gilly's loover*. What a funny old crowd.

One more tale about Tater Billy. I don't know all the details about this next tale, but I think I have got most of it. Several years ago, one of Tater Billy's old *vardo* wheels, like me, got a little worse for wear, so Tater decided to get someone to repair the old *bowler*. Billy could not get anyone local to do the job. Perhaps the local boys knew what Tater Billy was like, so Tater had to take the old *bowler* into Norwich to have it mended. As you may know, be it a front wheel or a back wheel, they are all very heavy. The only way Tater Billy could get it to Norwich was by train. Tater had a job to get old Milly into the sidecar on the motorbike, so no way could he get a *vardo bowler* in it. So Tater rolled it to Holt railway station and put the wheel and himself on the *ratler* (train). I don't know where in Norwich Tater took it. After a time the wheel was repaired and Tater went again to Norwich to collect his *vardo bowler*. Can you imagine poor old Tater Billy rolling a heavy wheel through Norwich, to the station, then again from Holt station to Grove Road? At last Tater arrived home, but home to what? When old Tater Billy staggered up the steps of his old wagon, he was not greeted in a friendly way by Milly...the old *mort* was savage. She accused poor old Tater of being a long time in Norwich. She thought he was after some of those old Norwich *lubnies* (ladies of the night). Christ, before Tater could reply, old Milly hit him over the head with a heavy old copper *hotchimengri* (frying pan), and she nearly *mullered* him. They were an odd couple – you wouldn't want to meet that pair in the dark or the daylight. If they could not find anyone else to get wrong with, they would get wrong with each other. What a pair of *dinolos* (fools).

There is one more little tale I will tell you about old Milly. Go on, you can't wait, can you? At the moment, Tater Billy and Milly are getting star billing. If you bought my last book, you may remember I talked about Loren Guyton, the *givengro* (farmer) from White House Farm, Knapton. He was well *motty* most of the time. Several years ago, Loren was in the Angel Hotel in North Walsham. He was with a *mush* by the name of Tammy Wright, who was Loren's 'chauffeur'. Mother and Edgie were there, along with lovely Milly, who was drinking a stout. Old Milly was sitting next to Edgie and we were all getting a little *motty*. Anyhow, what happened was old Milly said to Edgie, "I had to have my old *grai* put down as he was getting very old... that would be about a year ago." Milly continued, "I still have the trolley and the harness in my shed over at Holt; they're in good order. If you would like them, brother-in-law, I will give them to you." I think a few years ago old Milly would do a bit of *tatting* (rag collecting) around Holt. What would those old 'posh blue bloods' think of that now? If old Milly was still *tatting*, they would have her put down. By the way, that would maybe be a good thing!

Anyway, Edgie did not want Milly's turnout, and he did not want to get involved with her. Also, back in the day, they were not making much *loover*. Loren Guyton had overheard the conversation and he was keen on buying the turnout, but Loren could not get Milly's attention so he leaned over and tapped on her knee. She could, if she had had an ounce of sense, have taken good *loover* off Loren. Cor, she went ballistic – she cried out and the whole pub heard her. She shouted, "That dirty old man just put his hand up my dress!" She went bananas – she was about to call in the *gavvers* (police) and have poor old Loren *stiffed* (arrested). The poor old *motty mush* meant no harm at all. We all had a job to cool old Milly down. She was one of the easiest people on the planet to get wrong with. I don't know who had Milly's old cart and harness.

The last time I saw Milly, she was with her sister Daisy. They were in Swaffham cemetery in the Sixties. Both were attending their brother Albert's funeral. Everything was going fairly smoothly until they lowered poor Albert into the *mulleno hev* (grave). That's when the two 'nice' sisters wanted to jump in! They were shouting and wailing – it takes all sorts! Some mothers do have them.

A Roadside Reverie

I have noticed on several occasions that with Romanies, you can be drinking and laughing togetther, having a good time and there is always one who will upset the apple cart, kick off and go divvy. It happens very often; it must be the Oriental urge which is still in the *ratti* (blood). It seems it comes on when the old *scimish* kicks in. I think what we are dealing with here is an old, fairly primitive type of people. As we know, Romanies are most certainly Oriental in their DNA, and I think most Romanies of today still have traces of this inherent makeup. It would be a very sad loss if this – I will describe it as an aggressive nature – was to be totally removed from their makeup. Romanies are not a violent race: murders and violent crimes are not part of their culture. In fact, I know no other race whose people have such a total loving nature for their children. Their strong beliefs in the framework of their family is simply unique and unequivocal. I think only people of Italian descent can come only somewhat close to the beliefs in family harmony and endeavour of the Romanies.

A Romany is very quick to anger, but I think this is because of all the years he had to endure persecution. Suspicion and hate – they have made him what he is today. However, a Romany soon forgets and is quick to respond with laughter and mirth. I think if you were able to peel away layers of Romany traits and faults, you would find not a timid person, but a person worthy of love and compassion with a strong aptitude. For endless years, he has been provoked, harassed and persecuted. Some have even tried to exterminate him; but, my friends, like an old fox lying in his burrow, he will not go away...and why should he? Let's all rejoice in the strength of the Romany's resolution to survive and survive he will.

If at any time you are driving or maybe taking a gentle stroll down an old Norfolk country lane, just stop and look at the old overgrown common, close your eyes for a few minutes and listen. Maybe you will hear young *chies* and *chals* (girls and boys) playing amongst those old gorse bushes; maybe, just maybe, you will hear the tapping as an old Romany *mush* makes his *tograms* or you may hear the clink of the chains as a grazing *grai* reaches out for that extra bit of *chaw* (grass). Be careful, stand aside – what's that, what can I hear? The noise is getting louder – much, much louder! My word, I don't believe this! It's a large, brightly painted old kite wagon...it has a *sider* (horse) tied to the *sharps*, to train it and to assist the other horse to pull the *vardo*.

Look out, here comes another wagon. My god, it's a Bill Wright Ledge wagon. Bill Wright was one of the best, if not the best, wagon makers in England. He was renowned for his Bow-Tops. After the Ledge wagon comes a flat Bradford trolley loaded up with shouting, happy *chies* and *chals*. Their skin is the colour of copper and they are a raggedy ramble of a bunch. Driving this turnout is old Butty Lamb's *mort* (wife), Mary-Ann. Whatever you do, don't get in her way, or she will have a few choice words for you. Here they come – old Butty is driving the kite wagon. It gets its name because it is a kite shaped. The second wagon is driven by a Romany *rakla*. It might even be my mother, Mary, I just don't know...is this a dream or is it reality?

The sun is reflecting on gold *fawnees* (rings) and bright *kaun fawnees* (earrings). These people have that dark, dusty skin and very bright *yoks* (eyes) and white *stackus* (teeth). Onto the old common they draw. The *grais* have come a long way today. Old Butty, in the last few days, has not been allowed to *hatch* (stop) for a moment, but at last he knows this old common is out of the way of large country estates or *yogger mushes* (gamekeepers). If he's lucky he will, perhaps, be able to *hatch* for a week or more. He can rest his *grais*, make some *tograms* (linen pegs) for his *mort* and *chies* to blue (sell). He may also *fake* (mend) some *mush's* umbrellas and get a *bitti loover* (small bit of money) together.

This is the time when the whole family regroup: have a little peace and quiet after the turmoil of the last few days. Theirs is not an easy life; it's tough. The stress saps your strength and devitalises you. Sometimes you just need an inner sanctuary for a few days. We Romanies are fighting life's daily battles, and all we want is to belong...to live to enjoy the open spaces. But it will, my friend, be years before this is a reality. Maybe it will never happen.

Is this a mirage? I just don't know. Sometimes when you have a dream you do not want to wake up! What's happening on this old common? I do not want to approach too closely; it's almost like walking up to a dog. Is he friendly? Will he bite? I do not know, so I will just stand here and watch. The old *grais* have pulled the heavy old wagons onto the common and they are steaming! It has been a long journey today, and they deserve a rest and a bite of that lovely green *chaw*. Butty is backing his large, old coloured cob back so the old wagon is out of sight from the *drom*. He will also do the same with the others – off with the *straps* (harness), give the old *grais* a brush down using a nice handful of *cas* (hay), then turn them out on their twenty foot chains. A little *pani* (water), maybe a handful or two of corn later, and they will be as right as ninepence.

The *sharps* (shafts) are supported on wooden stands which Butty unties from under the sharps, then after wiping down the *straps* they are placed to hang on the sharps. From inside the wagon Butty pulls out a pair of ornate 'S' shaped steps and places them between the *sharps* so old Mary-Ann can get into the wagon and get all of her 'crown derby' china, plus her silver family photo frames all depicting photos of her large family of twelve *chavies* – eight *chals* and four *chies*. After she has set out her *covels* (things) in the old wagon she gets her old *saster kaba cosh* (iron kettle hook) which she uses to suspend a *kekauvi* (kettle) over the *yog* (fire). She also gets her iron pot where her *puvengros* (spuds) and *mass* (meat) will be thrown in to cook away. There is nothing in this world that could beat a bit of *scran* (food) cooked in this way.

A rare find through Facebook. The Lamb family hatching on Ridlington Common with the author's grandmother, Mary Ann Lamb (wife of Butty Lamb), in the centre with the large hat and the author's mother, Mary, sitting on the steps of the wagon behind the lad with cap.

The *chavies* all have their tasks to do; some will find some *cosh* for the *yog*, and maybe others will take an old pram which is stowed on the trolley. They will also take two milk churns and go and see if they can *mong* (beg) a little *pani* from some old *Gorgio* for drinking and cooking. Most country folk do not mind the Romanies; they know they only come around this way maybe once or twice a year and most are fairly friendly...even old Butty's *mort*, Mary-Ann, is fairly friendly this morning. This makes a change.

There are *needis hatching* (travellers stopping) on the old common. It's most impolite to approach other families if they are *scraning* (eating). You wait 'til later, and only then can you approach them. Most Romanies will know each other. It's also customary to have a wash and put on your better *togs* when you visit someone even though it's only on a bit of old common. *Chavies* will not be tolerated at these evening meetings, but they have their chores to do. When sitting down at a *yog*, women will be expected to sit with their legs under their bodies and not to show off their legs and it is a mortal sin in the Romany world to let down or comb your hair or brush it in the company of men. Nor may she walk in front of men...always behind.

Sometimes around the *yog* someone will produce a *bosh* (violin) or maybe a mouth organ and some hearty sing song will be heard or maybe they will just talk and ask one another where other families are *hatching* (staying). On the Romany grapevine everyone knows where everyone else is. It's better than the Royal Mail. In summertime, as it's the time of year when the Romanies are on the *drom*, they will pull an old tarpaulin around the wagon and lay a few bags of *kas* (hay) down, then over go whitney blankets of the finest quality and a better *woodrus* (bed) will be very hard to find in the kingdom of a King, Maybe before he went to bed, he may have sneakily *puved his grais* (put his horses) in a nearby field. He then would have to be up at first light to get his *grais* off before the old *givengro* (farmer) *diks* (sees) them. For a while the women and the oldest *chies* would go out *calling* (selling), taking with them large willow *kipsies* (baskets). Maybe they would sell *tograms* or trade old *mushes* (umbrellas), sometimes taking them in for part exchange and getting a bit of *loover*. The old broken *mushes* they had exchanged would be repaired to be *fenced* (sold) another day. If they had found the right kind of *Gorgio*, who look like they have *loover*, they would do a bit of *dukkering* (telling fortunes). They would have a false bottom in their large *kipsies* to hold the stuff they had *monged*, maybe a few *puvengros* (spuds) and a few *yoros* (eggs). Sometimes old Butty would come along with his trolley and pick them up or they would walk, buying a bit of *scran* (food) on a daily basis. When at last all the *buty* (work) was done and there were no more chores to do, they might spruce themselves up and go to a local cinema or down to a village *kitchema* if the *kitchema mengro* (landlord) would serve them.

Since he's been on the old common, Old Butty has spotted a nice thick-set coloured *tit* (mare) belonging to old Wisdom Smith. Butty draws over to old Wisdom's *vardo* and starts to *rokker* (talk) to him.

"How you doing, Wisdom?" he asks.

"I ain't too bad, Butty," says Wisdom.

"What do you know, that old *tit* over there looks a bit *wafti* (bad)," says Butty.

"You old *minge*, Butty, you don't know a *custi grai* (good horse) when you see one," replies Wisdom. "Have you gone blind in your *yoks* - that little hoss could pull your old kite wagon off his bit of common with the brake on."

"You are full of *kinder*, Wisdom, it could not pull an old *canni* off a nest."

"Why are you asking me about it if you think it's *wafti*, Butty?"

"Look you here, Wisdom," and old Butty spits his baccy juice, nearly hitting old Wisdom. "I'll tell you what I'll do, I'll take that old *grai* off your hands before the RSPCA man sees it; it's as thin as my old *mort*."

"What, you mean Mary-Ann? Butty, your old gal don't look too thin to me, she's as fat as a *hotchi-witchi* (hedgehog)."

"How many shillings for that worn out old *grai*, Wisdom?"

"Butty," Wisdom said, spitting baccy juice between Butty's Luton boots, "you have not got enough *loover* to buy that little mare."

"Tell you what I'm going to do, Wisdom; I will give you fifteen *bars* (pounds) for that old *tit* and – my god – I don't know what my old *mort* Mary-Ann will say. She will think I am a *dinolo* (fool)."

"Butty," cried old Wisdom, "I will *muller* that *tit* before I take fifteen *bars*. I tell you what I will do; I swear on my *chavies'* lives I will take twenty-five *bars*, and not a shilling less."

Butty responded, "I tell you what Wisdom, give me out two bars for luck and throw in your old 'lurcher' over there, and then I will have a deal with you."

"Christ, Butty, you are as tight as a drum; that little lurcher is the best *shooshi* (rabbit) catcher in Norfolk."

Butty could see old Wisdom would not bend so he said, "I tell you what I will do, I will toss you fifteen *bars* or twenty *bars*."

Old Wisdom could not resist a challenge. Butty threw up a gold sovereign, and old Wisdom called 'heads' and won. Cor, old Butty swore,

"You old *minge*, that's the dearest old *grai* I ever bought!"

Then, in true Romany style, they both hit hands to bind the deal. There was a lot of shouting but old Butty knew he had got himself a good *grai*. I stood quietly watching all this – the noise, the bustle, the thrill of the deal. I just stood in complete amazement and awe; what had I just witnessed as I stood there in a state of wonder?

I was rudely awakened by the loud blast of a lorry horn, a screech of brakes and a fellow in a large juggernaut. He shouted to me, "You want to get on the side of the road, you bloody idiot, I nearly ran you over. What the hell are you looking at? There's only an empty old common there." I slowly woke from the musty haze and I never again saw old Butty Lamb and Wisdom Smith. I would have liked to know if old Butty caught many *shooshis* with his lurcher, and what did old Mary-Ann say about Butty buying the coloured *grai*?

The Lamb children circa 1905: Ada, Daisy, 'Coddie', Albert, Mary (the author's mother) & Archie Lamb

Such weird and wonderful characters – you will see them no more unless you are very lucky or maybe see them in a dream or in a mirage. As you can see, Romanies like nothing better than to have a *chop* (deal); it's in their *ratti*. Whatever a Romany owns, be it a good *grai* or even his own *vardo* he will have a *chop* for it, sometimes coming off second best. All deals are noisy affairs with much shouting and the slapping of hands. In all deals, if you sell, you must give back to the buyer what's known as luck money. So sometimes, even if you have had a *wafti* deal you still have to part with *loover*.

*

As I said in my last book, the Romany *raklas* were the ones who controlled the *kissi-doris* (purse strings). I, myself, think this is because in days gone by, the *mush* was quite a lazy soul, preferring for the *raklas* to do the *buty* (work). Then I think that the *raklas* earning *loover* must have thought, "We have earned it, let's try and keep it and spend it wisely." The Romany *mush*, for all his shouting and boasting, was largely kept by his *mort*, so any decision making had to pass before her. The women ruled the roost, so to speak. Some of these old Romany *raklas* acquired some real wealth and power, enabling them to run and rule their clan of kinsfolk. Like poor old 'Tater Billy' Hudson – he could not come up with a good enough excuse for being late, and that's when old Milly hit him over the *shero* (head) with the copper frying pan.

True Romanies would also look after their old and aged parents. In my 77 years, I cannot remember a Romany putting a loved one into a care home. It's totally unheard of in the Romany world. They care for one another to the end of time. Another thing I will tell you is this: if by chance a mother *mullered*, thus leaving young *chavies*, other Romany *raklas* would take them and bring them up just like they were their own, giving them all the love and care that they deserved.

A Couple Of Lessons In Dealing

Look, I don't know about you, but this old book is getting a little on the sad side, Reader. Let me try and cheer you up! Christ, I am starting to get a little sick of all this writing. It reminds me of when I had done something *wafti* (bad) at school, and the old teacher would make me stay behind to do a load of writing as a punishment. It feels that way now!

Oh, by the way, did I tell you about 'Squiggles Taylor'...I think he got a mention in my last book? He was (or so we thought) an old mate of my father, Edgie, but you could not trust Squiggles. He would take a piece of *morro* (bread) from a workhouse child. I think this next tale was just after the Second World War. Christ, I just remembered something else about Squiggles – I think he was stationed in Egypt in the war. He was probably selling sand to them Arabs! Anyway, he was told his old *stackus* (teeth) weren't too good, so the Army made him a set. However, it seems he could not get on with them. When he was coming back home from Egypt, the old *stackus* were playing him up, so old Squiggles threw them overboard into the Mediterranean Sea and never wore teeth again.

He was a bit like me; I had trouble with my own ivories! I had two sets made: the first set made me look like a goofy character from The Dick Emery Show. The next set cost me over £700 and I could not get on with them, so I put them away in a drawer in my office. One day my old *mort* Hazel cried out to me. I did not take much notice of her, because she's always bloody crying out – old women, they send you around the bend! Anyway, she cried: "What's that old dog got out there on the lawn?" The dog was a Siberian Husky that belongs to my son Rodney. F**k me, that old *juk* had gotten my *stackus* and was chewing them up! They cost me 700 *bars*! So, Reader, when you happen to see me looking a little gummy, don't ask me where my teeth are or I will tell you the f*****g *juk* ate them.

Christ, Mike, you started to tell us about Edgie's old mate Squiggles and you finished up talking about Siberian Huskies eating your ivories. Right, let's try to get back on track.

After the war my mother decided she would like to take up a bit of driving, so she bought herself a little Singer 8hp car and started to learn how to drive it. Anyway, Mother could drive any old *grai*, but not the Singer car. At the time there was a good demand for old cars. It being just after the war, farmers could not buy farm trailers, so they would buy up old motor axles and make their own trailers for the farms. Mother sold the little *drag* (car) to a local farmer near us at Honing. He was a nice old boy and was well pleased with the deal. But, Reader, get your lugholes around this – Squiggles got to hear that Mother had sold the car to the farmer and he went into action. Squiggles's boss at Black Cat Garage in North Walsham made trailers and they wanted the old car. Anyway, Squiggles dropped in on the farmer one day. The farmer said to Squiggles, "What do you want?" Squiggles said, "I have come to take away that old Singer car."

"You bloody won't be taking that away, I want it for the axles," replied the farmer.

"You are in deep trouble," said Squiggles.

"What do you mean?" the farmer asked.

Squiggles said, "Edgie Harmer *chored* (stole) that old Singer car and the police are looking for it."

Christ, the old farmer was angry. He said, "The dirty little c**t, Edgie nicked it; take it away."

Squiggles paid the old farmer back what Mother had sold it for and took it to his boss. Squiggles got a good drink out of it.

Several weeks later Mother and Edgie called up the old *givengro* and asked him if he had anything to sell, and Christ he went into orbit, calling Edgie and Mother all the names under the sun. Mother and Edgie had a job to calm him down and explain what Squiggles had done. The farmer at last could see that he had been outsmarted by Squiggles. Who on this planet would want a mate like Squiggles? He would have the laces out of your boots – no, he wouldn't – he would have your boots as well.

Let's leave Squiggles for a while and talk about a different subject. I could fill half this book talking a about Squiggles, heaven forbid! In my last book, I wrote about a lovely old character, old Tommy Manes from Mundesley. He was the *mush* who went around the *kenners* (houses) sharpening *churis* (knives) and *catches* (scissors), etc. The first time I met him I was a little *thrashed* (frightened); it must have been in the Sixties. Mother and I were doing a bit of billing down at Mundesley where old Tommy lived. Billing, as I mentioned earlier, is when you leaflet a row of *kairs* (houses) with cards specifying what you are after, such as *tats*, *scraps*, antiques, etc. Anyway, we had laid a fair few around Mundesley and we were picking them up and buying stuff that the old *monistas* (women) had found for us. I went round a bungalow and picked up my bill, and the lady said she had found me some *covels* (things). She had a nice few sacks of *tats* and a *gunner* (sack) with a good lot of old pewter teapots in it. I put my *vast* (hand) into my *putsi* (pocket) and gave her a few clods (coins), then I loaded the stuff on to the old truck I was driving and carried on down the *tober* to pick up more things.

Just then, on an old bike with a grindstone fixed to the handlebars came a *mush*, shouting and going ballistic at me. I was getting a little bit nipped up, being fairly young and immature. If my Mother had not come out of a *stigur* (gate) at the time, I think I would have been laying on my back, probably with a black *yok* (eye).

"You have just robbed my old woman, you little b*****d; you have taken my pewter and *tats*!" raged Tommy.

Mother shouted to him, "Keep your *miltog* (shirt) on, that's my boy!"

Old Tommy apologised to Mother. He said, "I did not know he was your boy."

Anyway, he cooled down, my mother gave Tommy a little more *loover* and he was alright about it after that. Old Tommy went back home and found us some metal up and from that day onwards until the sad day he passed away, Tommy and I got on with one another 'like a house on fire'. Sadly, old Tommy has passed away, but I sometimes see his daughter Topsy. She is the same age as me and still lives at Mundesley. Anyone who crossed old Tommy Manes would have to watch out, but he was one of the nicest people you would want to meet. I think I am right in saying that when old Tommy came to live at Mundesley he, like I, lived in an old railway carriage up near Charlie Payne's farm in Mundesley.

*

Right, Reader, here's another one; I know you like a little yarn or two. Have you ever been waiting for something or someone? When the old urge comes along (you must know what I mean), you want a *mutra* (pee) and you just cannot find anywhere to do it. Of course you have – it happens to all of us. It happened to me several years ago at Lower Street, Southrepps, down this old village lane with houses on both sides and not a tree in sight. My mother and I were calling the old *kairs* for *tats*, and I had just finished my row of *kairs*. I had bought a few *gunners* (bags) of *tats*. I was sitting in my old *moulder* (lorry) waiting for my mother, who had gone round a house. Cor, my old bladder was full – I had to keep stamping my feet on the old lorry floor. Christ, was I in pain. Where was my mother, she'd been 'round that old house for ages.

Coming up the road very slowly was an old coal lorry delivering his coal to nearly all the houses. Christ, where was she? I couldn't hold it much longer – I was soon going to piss myself, but she still didn't come. I was in total agony. The coalman at last got near me and said,

"Your mother, Mary, is shouting about you."

"What do you mean? Where is she? Where is she?"

"She's sitting down the bottom of the road on a big heap of old rags, smoking her Craven A cigarette. She thinks you have got lost."

"Bloody hell" I cried.

I had been sitting outside this old *kair* for ages, having nearly pissed myself, and she is down the bottom of the road. How did she get there? What had happened? She must have carried on down the road behind the *kenners* (houses), causing me to miss her. I drove down to her, threw the old *tats* on the *moulder*, and drove away from the *kairs* and jumped over the *bor* (hedge). I was in so much pain, I had a job to start: I also had a bloody job to stop! To put it mildly, I was a little bit 'pissed' off!

And Did Those Hooves...

Back to the Romanies of old. Today you still have a few old *Gorgios* (non-Romanies) driving an old *tit* (mare) out on a Sunday afternoon. They drive a few miles, stop, pull up to a pub, have a drink, carry on a few more miles and then wander home. They think they are kings of the road. How sad it is that the day of the horse has gone. I am not talking about thoroughbred race horses, bred mostly by some rich oil Sheikh – I am talking about working horses which made Great Britain great. Like everything, there is a time and a place; alas, the driving horse is only a sad reminder of its glorious past in the equine world. What if they were still around today, the creatures that Stubbs and Munnings depicted in their fine equine paintings? Old *tits* are hardly able to trot ten miles an hour, let alone twenty miles an hour. Yes, it's like true old Romanies – they've had their day...they're finished. England's former glories were built not as people would have us believe, upon steam, but on horsepower. Remember Waterloo – that noble iron duke upon his noble steed Copenhagen. Remember 'The Charge of the Light Brigade': not just any horses, but truly noble beasts that man will see no more.

Reader, to give you some idea of the quality of the humble horse, I will take you back to my Mother and Father, Mary and Edgie Harmer. Many years back, they had to go down to Colchester in Essex to fetch home a sister of mine who had been staying with Edgie's brother. Don't ask me why she was staying there – I just don't know – but to Colchester they had to go to fetch her back to the railway carriage here at North Walsham. This was a distance of about 81 miles. That *grai* of Edgie's was no Shergar, just one of his everyday *tits*. They set off, not in a light Irish gig, but with an everyday working trolley. Believe me, Reader, they reached Colchester in a day, bearing in mind they had a few *shants* (pints) on the way and they also stopped to *pani* (water) and *bait* (feed) the horse. From North Walsham to Colchester in today's terms would be a good drive with a *drag* (car), so you see, Reader, what I am trying to show you is that even little old Edgie Harmer had a *tit* that could trot over the stones, so to speak. There was a time when this great country was dependent on the horse - in field, in industry and in battle, but now, if we all open our *yoks* and look around, we find that the time has all but passed for many things, including horses and Romanies. You cannot truly resurrect the past, but, if you can keep all these memories alive within yourself, you will be the better for it.

Now, while we are on the subject of lost things, perhaps I had better tell you about my uncle Winks Lamb and his trip to Colchester. You will see what I mean, Reader, just travel with me awhile.

Down here at North Walsham lived a *mush* by the name of Jimmy Jordan; I think he was related to Ben Jordan, the car dealer from Coltishall. I also think that the Jordans had a little Romany *ratti* in them. They were loosely related to the Waterfield family and you can't get any purer *ratti* than that.

This would have been around the 1950s, when Jimmy's son Ralph Jordan had been called up for the army. He was going to be a *kooli* (soldier) and was stationed in the army barracks at Colchester. Ralph had just finished his training and was about to be posted overseas. His father Jimmy and Winks were on the old *scimish* (beer) in the Lord Nelson pub one afternoon in North Walsham and I can tell you, the old boys were getting well *motty* (drunk). Some folk, when they get a few *shants* (pints) into themselves, behave in different ways. Some get happy and others become sad. Jimmy was of the latter persuasion. He became maudlin and started to think about his son, who I believe he had never treated too well. Jimmy was filled with remorse and melancholy. He knew in the next few days his son would be posted abroad and wondered when he would see him again. So Jimmy and Winks decided that they would set off that very same day and go to Colchester so Jimmy could console his son though first they had another drink and waited until Mrs Grimes, the landlady, called time on the afternoon drinkers. It was already fairly late in the day when the two old *motty* boys finally began their epic journey to Colchester.

They travelled in Jimmy's battered old army truck in which Jimmy would *hawk* firewood around North Walsham, but the pair of lads didn't just drive there like most normal people would. Instead, it was more like a jolly boys' outing for this pair, who stopped at *kitchemas* en route. Somehow they managed to get to Suffolk. They spotted a nice *ginger beer shop* (pub) and decided to sample the local brew, which they did with wild abandon, pouring the amber nectar down their *curlos* (throats). Now in this *kitchema* were several old Suffolk boys having a few *shants*. Jimmy, on hearing how these Suffolk folk spoke, started laughing as he thought it was very funny. Jimmy was always taking the p**s out of anyone when he had a little *scimish* inside him. The old Suffolk boys were getting a little sick of Jimmy Jordan. Winks could see there might be trouble so he took stock of the situation and explained to the Suffolk boys that their speech sounded funny, as our Norfolk speech did to them. He told them not to take any notice of his drunken mate because he was a *dinolo* (fool). Somehow Winks managed to cool them down and then everyone got on well together.

Winks and Jimmy remained in the pub until late. After closing time, outside the pub, they said their farewells to their new-found drinking buddies and climbed into the old truck to *sove* (sleep) until the morning, when they would resume their journey. It was not too long before daybreak came and Jimmy drove the old truck out of the pub yard on the road to Colchester. As they were driving, Winks said to Jimmy,

"I think we are going the wrong way! It's those electric pylons; they should be on the other side of the road." Jimmy said,

"Hang on, we will soon be in Colchester."

It was not long when they saw lots of houses which they thought was Colchester. It was not: it was bloody Norwich! Jimmy and Winks never did manage to get to their destination and Ralph never did get a hug and a few kind words from his Dad. I think the old amber nectar got the better of those two old boys. And to think Edgie and Mary had found Colchester with the old *grai*! Good job Jimmy was not a bus driver – where would he have taken the passengers?

A Turkey Tale

I told you we lived in an old railway carriage down here on Spa Common. I had some lovely times down there. There were always people coming and going, always someone dropping in for a talk or maybe to have a deal with us. We always had a good range of livestock with the two *grais* and the pigs, goats, chickens, turkeys and rabbits. I remember one time when I was not too old and still at school...down by the riverbank I found a turkey nest. I eased the savage old turkey off the nest and *chored* (stole) her eggs. I took them home and Mother set them down under an old broody hen. Anyway, Mother hatched off six little turkeys. (Not my Mother, the hen, you fool!) There were four little hen turkeys and two stags, which we brought up. Before long these turkeys were getting very big and at night time they roosted up a tree close to the old railway carriage.

Well, my Mother used to smoke a fair number of Craven A cigarettes and she always had a cough. It was summertime and the windows were open where Edgie and Mother slept. In the night Mother started to cough. Christ, you should have heard them old gobblers – every time Mother barked out, the old turkeys let out a holler. Edgie said, "I have had a gut full of this. There's my old woman coughing her guts out in the middle of the night and there's them bloody turkeys crying out, keeping me awake. What a place to live. If it's not my old mort, it's them f*****g turkeys. Roll on Christmas, when someone puts them turkeys on their plates."

The turkey story still doesn't end there. Mother fattened them up and sold five of them for the old yuletide feasts. The last remaining stag – a monster – we killed and dressed out. Mother then went and bought several books of raffle tickets and started to sell tickets for a Christmas turkey. She was selling them for half a crown a pop, which was good *loover* back then. She took loads of *loover* for the stag turkey by the night of the grand Christmas draw, which was held at The Anchor pub here on Spa Common. Someone pulled out of the hat the winning ticket: the winner was a Mr Brooks. Old Charles Brooks, who ran the Spa Common next door to The Anchor had won it...or so he thought! Someone said, "The winner is Mr Brooks." Old Brooky tried to claim his lovely Christmas turkey. However, my mother didn't like the old *mush* and quickly said, "It's not you who has won the old turkey, but another Mr Brooks from Norwich." Poor old Brooky's face dropped and he was done out of his prize. The stunts they pulled years ago – you simply could not trust anyone. Poor old Brooky thought he was going to have a cheap Christmas dinner. Poor old boy!

A Riot Of Romanies

We had another large event down at the old railway carriage, which (as I told you) was called 'The Windy City'. Of course I told you! What have you forgotten already! 'Large event' makes it sound more like a carnival than a funeral. Anyhow, poor old Mary-Ann Lamb had just passed away, God bless her. It was, I think, about 1958, as you should know if you are reading this book and taking notice of what I am trying to tell you! For Christ's sake, pay attention! Poor old Mary-Ann Lamb was, I think, about 87 years old. She was my mother's old *dai* (mother) and the *mort* of Butty Lamb, my Mother's *dadrus* (dad), who had passed away in 1945. Old Mary-Ann, having a large family and being well known to Romanies all over Norfolk and other counties, was much respected. It was therefore only natural that there would be a good turn out for this Romany interment.

As it was to be held in North Walsham and we had plenty of space down at 'The Windy City', Mother thought she would have the gathering of the clan down here. Romanies turned up from all parts of the county as well as from other counties. I can still remember most of the families – on that day there was a lot of good Romany *ratti*. How I wish I could see them all again and just be able to *rokker* (talk) to them. Like I have said before, you can't turn back life's clock. Just to see these fine folk for one last time would be truly amazing, like something from heaven (itself a utopia of Romanies), never to be seen again. By the way, Reader, you can get an exaltation of larks, a wisp of snipes, and a gaggle of geese, but what do you call a gathering of Romanies?

I can see them so clearly; the vision is fresh in my *yoks*. What's this noise? It's a large old Bedford lorry pulling into our *puv* (field)...who is it? Why, it's old Minne Slender, the one on the front cover of my first book, Kaka Rokker Romany, and so she deserves to be. You can't get any *kaulo ratti* (black blood) better

Sidney Waterfield in all his glory.

than this. She is being driven in the old *moulder* (lorry) by her grandson John Lamb, Winks Lamb's *chal*. Also in the *moulder* is Minne's daughter, Collena Brown, another true Romany. It's a feast for one's yoks – it's like a cavalcade of vehicles. Next rolling in is a large black Austin 16 Saloon carrying Sidney and his mort, Nigger Kidd from Briston. The *tomfoolery* (jewellery) dazzles your *yoks*. Sidney is holding an ornate cane smothered in silver and his Luton *chokkers* (boots) shine like ice. Next, who is this? It's Mother's sister, Daisy Lamb from East Dereham and Milly Hudson from Holt. Whatever you do, don't wind these two *raklas* up the wrong way or you will be in big trouble. These two will get wrong with the stones in the road. I don't know if Tater Billy was there with Milly. I don't think he was; he was probably at Grove Lane in Holt, looking after those two old wagons of his in case some old shepherd came and p****d over the wheels!

It's amazing: they are still rolling in. Here comes Bert Lamb, Mother's brother, and Lilly. He is driving a very large van. He needs it, because he has a large family of *chies* and *chals*, some of whom are tiny babies. I don't believe this – in through the gate have walked Manny and Sidney Waterfield. You cannot get better Romanies than these. Just to hear them *rokker* (talk) is like magic – the Romany coming from their *muis* (mouths) is like pure liquid gold. How very sad that they are not still here... long may we remember them.

Who is this? Why, it is my cousin Stanley Gray from Attleborough, bringing his poor old *dai* (mother), Ada Gray, Mother's oldest sister. A tall, proud Romany, her *rom* (husband) Charlie Gray left Ada but she did a good job bringing up her chals and chies. I think her chals were there: yes they are there. I can remember like it was yesterday. There's tall Felix Gray, not so tall Russell Gray, and let's not forget Gilly Gray and Harry Gray, all wearing snap brim trilbies. They are proud Romanies and so they have the right to be. This is a sad day but it is also a day when you are proud to be a Romany. All my mother's other brothers are there. Poor Winks – he is the youngest, and he was the last one living with his mother, Mary-Ann. He seems to be missing her the most. He spent years with her in that old Soham *vardo* at Catchpit Lane, North Walsham.

Winks's other brothers are here. There is Chinner (or Archie) from near Kings Lynn, Hobby Lamb, Daniel 'Butcher' Lamb and Albert – who is known as Petty – driving a smart Wolseley car. This man always has a good *drag* (car). Jinny, his wife, is with him. She, bless her, always rolls her own *tibloes* (cigarettes). Bob Lamb has also arrived all the way from Essex where he lives. He has two sons with him; one, like Ada Gray's son Charlie, is deaf and dumb, but they all stand in our old yard. Proud Romanies, they stand tall. This assembly is like royalty. I have not seen so many Romanies gathered in one place.

Sidney Kidd and Levi Blake shaking on a deal next to the River Eden in Appleby

Hello, who's this *mush* shouting and laughing? It's Arthur Kidd, old Sidney's *chal* from Saxthorpe. With him is his brother, Dougie Kidd. You never see them apart. There is his other brother, Mike Kidd. After the funeral and wake, Mike will be trying to buy something off these Romany mourners. After they have had a deal with Mike, they will be mourning a whole lot louder.

Left: Archie 'Chinner' Lamb and his brother, Albert. Right The Lamb family: Clockwise from top left: Ada, Mary (the author's mother), Albert and Milllie.

With the noise and the colours, the sheer atmosphere is breathtaking; but who have I missed out? Plenty, I would think, since this happened over sixty years ago. If any of you good Romanies are still out there and I have missed you out, I humbly apologise. Most have passed away onto that old green common in the sky. All is going peacefully. Just wait 'til later on when they get on that old *scimish*. There will be a few *chingaros* (quarrels) and some sore heads when they get *motty*.

Also at the funeral there were Popes, Gaskins, Browns, Leveridges and Wilsons – too many to remember. There was no traditional burning of the old wagon. My Uncle Winks was still living in the old wagon that his father Butty Lamb had built by Leonards of Soham in Cambridgeshire. There would be no fighting over any *loover*, because Mary-Ann had lived to a ripe old age and had spent her last gold sovereigns with old Lou Lancaster, the landlord of the Rising Sun inn! What a day. I would think without a shadow of a doubt that this was one of the biggest gatherings of Romanies in Norfolk. I was glad I was there. Sadly, most of these good folks have gone to their maker, just like you and I will. It's not a big deal – it will happen – but let's keep these wonderful folks in our fondest memories. That's the reason I am trying to write this *lil* (book), so some of you who did not know these folks can get a better understanding of their history and culture. Also I know that some of you, maybe – just maybe – will have a little Romany *ratti* in your veins, so you may have feelings for these amazing folks. They will never be forgotten, I am sure. Others will come along and strive to keep their memories afloat.

The Art Of The Deal

Come on, Reader, it's time I took you with me to show you how I operate. We are going out there to buy a bit of *rust* or anything else we can *kin* (buy). Come on, I haven't got all day! I wonder if I have done right by taking you with me. Jump in my old *moulder* (lorry). Christ, what are you doing? Give the bloody old door a good bang, then it might shut! That's better, let's get up the *drom*, or it will be dinner time before we go.

It's a nice morning to have a deal. People are in a better mind if it's a nice day. Let's bloody hope so! Hold tight: here comes old Ikey Wright down the road. He never looks where he is going, silly old sod. Behind Ikey will be a pack of *juks*. Ikey doesn't take them for a walk, but he takes them for a run behind his truck... what a carry on. He's got a half tidy little lurcher amongst them. She looks a good sort: I might try and buy that off Ikey when I run into him again. Blast me, Ikey has nearly run into me. You want to open your *yoks*, you old goat. Look where you are going! It takes something to have a deal with Ikey Wright. A few years ago my father, Edgie, asked Ikey what he wanted for a little bay pony which he had. Ikey said "Edgie, I want the biggest handful of notes that I can get." How can you deal with him?

My old *moulder* is nearly out of petrol, so I had better call in at Black Jack's garage on Spa Common. That's the trouble with these old *moulders*; you have to spend a load of money on them before you can earn a *nook* (penny). Edgie never had this trouble, as his old *tit* used to fill herself up with a bit of *chaw* (grass) and a little *pani* (water).

We pull in at Black Jack's garage, which looks like a *kinder kair* (shithouse). The garage consists of a large wooden shed with a nissen hut at the back. From a distance it looks like a prisoner of war camp. Stalag Spa Common! Black Jack has only one pump working, and the other one has a notice stuck on it made from a Kellogg's corn flake box. Out of Order. I would think the old *mush* has not got the *loover* to fill it up. As there is only one pump I have not got any choice: either I put this brand of juice into my old *moulder*, or I find myself another garage. I think I will stick with this one. Black Jack doesn't come out and serve you, you have to go and find him. What a carry on. "Are you about, Herbert?" I cry. His name is Herbert Chapman, but to everyone he is Black Jack (I wonder why). My God, he's laying under an old Humber Hawk car in a pit. It will take him ages to get out of there. I need to get up the *drom* and earn some *loover*. It will be dinner time before I get off Spa Common.

At last! Here he comes, and I can now see why they call him Black Jack. He's covered in oil and grease. He is as black as the ace of spades. Here he comes, without a smile on his *boat* (face). He keeps chewing peanuts. He gave up smoking and now eats about a 20 kilo bag of peanuts a week. I would think they cost more than the *tibloes* (cigarettes). "How much petrol you want?" he grunts. I wonder which charm school he went to? "How much is that petrol, Herbert?"

"You know how much it is, it says so on the pump!" He grunts, "It's four and sixpence a gallon."

Christ, this old petrol is getting dear, and I reply, "Put me ten bob's worth in. Herbert, by the way, have you got any old scrap batteries or scrap lying around? If you have I will try and have a deal with you." I knew you couldn't buy anything off this old *mush*; he was frightened I might earn two bob off him.

"No, I have not sorted anything out yet," he said.

Christ, I have been asking him for years. It's a pity my old *moulder* was low on fuel, because I would have bought it somewhere else. Anyway, I *pestered* (paid) him and I started to *jell up the tober* (go up the road).

Hold tight, Reader, we are off again. Are you glad you came with me for a ride? You won't be if I buy an old farm implement and you have to break it up with my 16lb hammer! You see I have not moved forward too much – no oxy cutting gear, and I am still using a 16lb hammer. I was only joking; I can still swing a *delomescro* (hammer). Along we go, past White Horse Common. There is old Dan Hudson, the one that Edgie caught. He never did pay old Dan all the *loover* for three *baulos* (pigs) he almost *monged* (begged) off him. "Are you alright Dan?" I shout through the open window. Dan waves to me. I think the old *mush* has forgotten about Edgie. I pull the old *moulder* up outside of the Cubbitt & Walkers mill at Ebridge. It's a big, old flour mill. I slip into the weighbridge office and see an old boy who I know. Well, sometimes if you can catch them right, they sometimes have a lot of paper sacks which fetch good *loover*. Unfortunately, today I am out of luck – old Manny Waterfield and his niece Collena have beaten me to it. No sacks for me! It would have been a good day to *cop* (get) something on your first call; see you mate! I tell the *mush* you can't win them all: pity you can't. Blast me, it's a hard old life at times, trying to earn a crust.

Never mind; let's get up the *tober* and try and find something else. I always think if you can have a deal at your first call, then the rest of the day will run more smoothly. I tell you what: it's bloody hot in this old *moulder*...you boil your socks off in summer and freeze your b******s off in winter. I start to draw into Bacton, which is not a bad little place. There are a fair few little smallholdings around here. I usually have a *touch* (deal) here. I pull into Peter Williamson's small farm. I can see Peter, who is running after a bloody huge white sow. There are about ten old sows in this open yard, and Peter has got a large syringe in his hand. At last, Peter corners the old sow in the yard and he gives it an almighty jab with the syringe. Christ, the old sow lets out! You would, too, if someone stuck that into you!

Peter climbs out of the yard, and he's panting away, trying to get his breath back. I say, "What are you doing?"

"Christ, Mike," he says, "them old sows of mine are a wild old bunch. I just turned some more sows in and they keep ripping their ears off; I have to inject them to calm the old sods down! By the way Mike, what are you after?"

"What have you got laying about, Peter? Have you got any old scrap?"

He says, "Let's walk up the road, onto my old *pygtle* (field) and we will have a look."

On the *pygtle* Peter has a tidy heap of *rust*. Amongst it I can *dik* (see) a few batteries and a bit or two of *smut* (brass). Peter is not too hard to deal with, so I finish up, paying him £2.10s. The batteries and the *smut* will come to that, thus leaving my scrap costing nicksas (nothing). Peter then says to me, "Who is that in your truck Mike?"

"I don't know him," I say "...he's just a reader of my book!"

Peter scratches his head. He must think that I am a brick short of a load, a *dinolo* (fool). We leave Peter and drive off.

A short distance up the *drom*, I am in Edingthorpe. I pull up at George Green's farm. He is the George Green who Hobby Lamb had bought the pictures off, in the Battle of Waterloo. They came from his father, old George Green. Hobby promised he would never sell them, but he *blued* (sold) them the next day in Stalham sale. George says to me,

"Have you seen Hobby? He's still got father's old pictures; he will never sell them." What a *dinolo*! "What are you buying up, Mike, scrap?"

"I am trying to, what have you got some laying around?"

"No, I have not got any. Old Bert Lamb cleared me out. But come you with me; I have something you might buy! Come in my barn, young Edgie!" Cheeky old sod!

George takes me into this old dark barn. Christ, it is dark.

"What do you think of that?" he says.

"What are you running on about? I can't see f**k all."

"The old cart, Mike."

My old *yoks* start to focus, and in the corner of the old barn I just see a half tidy old Norfolk dealer's cart. It is a bit on the heavy side, but a nice old *drag* (cart). I think to myself – I had better be a bit careful here – show too much interest and the old *loover* will go up.

"How long have you had that old bit of s**t in here, George?"

"Bit of s**t? Why, that's my Dad's old dealer's cart, and they tell me they are starting to make good prices at the moment," George cries.

"Ha, who told you that, George? They must have been on drugs! The old cart has seen better days," I say.

"So have you, young Edgie," said George. "What are you going to give me for that old cart?"

"Cor, George, I thought you were going to pay me to take it away." I could then see George getting a little waspy. "Tell you what, I will give you a fiver!"

"A fiver? I can't take that."

"'Course you can," I say.

"Give me a tenner and it's yours and that's a bargain," he says.

"It might be for you, George, but it won't be a bargain for me! Tell you what I will do, George, I will toss you for a fiver or eight pounds. If not, I'm off up the old road and you will have to keep it."

George looks me in the eye...I know he loves a gamble. "Go on young Edgie, throw her up!"

I spit on the old two bob bit and spin it. George calls heads, and it comes down tails: and I have a cheap little *dilly* (cart) for a fiver. I *pester* (pay) George and tell him I will pick it up later when I have emptied the *rust* from my old *moulder*. Right, that was a good morning's work. I don't often work afternoons, but I will get a mate of mine to help me to get the old cart home before someone tells the old *givengro* (farmer) that the cart is worth fifty pounds!

Right, Reader, I must now ask you to get out of my *moulder*. I might, if you are lucky, take you out another day. I must be a little careful – I don't want to learn you *Gorgios* too much. If I do, you will know as much as me, and we can't have that, can we?

My lifelong mate, Russell Farrow, is coming with me after dinner. By the way, Russell has a bit of Romany *ratti* in him. Russell is brother to Donny Farrow, and their old grandmother was a Gay, from a good Romany family. I draw home to 'The Windy City', that posh place down on Spa Common where you will find a lovely detached residence, our railway carriage. What are you laughing about, Reader? I bet you don't go on a train every day, but I do! I had a bit of *scran* (food), unloaded and sorted the *rust*. There was a nice bit of *smut* in there. Then I went into town and picked up Russell. He's a lovely old *chal*; alays willing to help me and never wanting large amounts of *loover*. We went to school at the same time, he's the salt of the earth. When we go back to the farm, George was out, which was a good job. We did not want him putting his oar in, plus when we pulled the old cart from the *gran* (barn) it was better than I thought. Like a couple of *dinolos* we had not taken any timbers to run the cart up onto my *moulder*, plus the old cart was on the heavy side. Russell said "what are we going to do?" "I tell you what Russell, lets pull the cart onto the road, put the cart behind it, you sit up on the moulder and hold the shafts and if I drive slowly we will get I home." Its not far, only about two miles. So off we go, slowly down the *drom*. All's going well until we come down the steep hill near Ikey Wright's Mill Farm. Ikey had already nearly hit me in his old truck this morning. Past the farm entrance we go, when Ikey comes flying out in his old truck. I had to brake. F**k, the old cart shot back! It pinned poor Russell to the front of the lorry. What a job! But the cart and Russell were alright. "That was close," Ikey shouted "will you take a fiver for that old cart?" I cried, "I won't take a £100 off of you! You should not be driving, Ikey. You are a menace on the road." At last we got the old cart home. Believe it or not, I put that old cart in a Michaelmas sale which Irelands held on the railway field at North Walsham. A Worstead farmer, Gavin Patterson was then starting to buy up old carts and wagons for his private collection and he bought my old cart for about £60. A good price then, it was in the early sixties. You might think that was a small amount, I had earned about fifty pounds. Back in that day a farm worker was only earning about fifteen pounds a week.

*

The next day I thought I would throw on my bit of *scrap* and a little metal which I had and have a drive up to Kings of Norwich and *fence* my load of *rust*. Everything was running smoothly and after about an hour, I drew into Kings scrap yard. Before I pulled on the weighbridge, I parked near the metal shed and out popped George Woods. I have told you before about him; he worked for Kings all his life. Christ, he was as sharp as a razor. You had to always drop him a tip or he would have the laces out of your *chokkers* (boots). He will still try to get your laces even though you have dropped him a tip – he's fly!

"Morning, George," I said.

"Hello, my son, how are you?"

"Not as well as you."

"What have you got me?" he asked. "You have got a nice bit of brass in that bag! Put it on the scales."

I didn't take my *yoks* off him! He then weighed my batteries, handed me my ticket, and I drove onto the weighbridge and down the yard. Anyway, I was sitting in my lorry in this wide yard when I heard an almighty bang. The next thing I knew, I was being dragged down the yard by a monster artic lorry. It was loaded up with tons of new steel. Christ, I was *thrashed* (frightened). The driver didn't realise he was pulling me down the yard.

After a while, the Kings yard foreman, Ralph Metcalf, saw what was happening and rushed in front of the lorry. The driver saw him and stopped. I thought truly to *dovel* (God) that I was *mullered*. Metcalf pulled the driver from the cab. I thought he was going to *coor* (fight) him. The dozy driver maintained he did not see me! Didn't see me? The yard is twenty yards wide! You should have seen my poor old *moulder*; most of the back was ripped off. After we unloaded it, we managed to rope it together and I somehow got it home. A few days later I phoned the company who owned the artic to claim compensation. The cheeky twat said to me,

"You want to get yourself a broker to deal with your insurances."

I said, "If *minges* like you did not run over me I would not want a broker!"

It went very well for me. I claimed for a new lorry body and they paid me good *loover* which I put in my *putsi* (pocket). Then I went and saw old Minnie Slender at her scrap yard and bought a good second-hand lorry body off her and had a nice bit of *vonger* (money) left in my *bin* (wallet).

*

When I first started in the scrap trade, you could get a good living out of it...but what happened was old *Gorgios* started to see what was going on. It did not take them long to see that, like us, they could take their scrap into a scrap yard and get good *loover* for it. Plus, the Transport Ministry brought in new rules for lorries. They had to be tested every year and there was a weight restriction on what you could carry. You also had to have an Operator's Licence – too much red tape, that's what killed it for a lot of us old *chals* . We used to be able to burn out old scrap cars: Christ, that was a hot and dirty job. I have been in situations where I have burnt out up to ten cars at a time. The black smoke you could see for miles away – we did not know then about global warming. Back then old cars contained a lot of scrap: plenty of brass and alloy, and also heavy engines and axles. They were the good old days which we will not see again.

Several years ago over at Sutton, near Stalham, a nice family by the name of Grimes had a large market garden with a lot of old glass houses on the site. This was in the Sixties. I think the family had sold or was about to sell the site for housing.

Anyway, my uncle Winks Lamb and I bought a large quantity of scrap from these people. The old *mush* was sweet and we had a good deal with him. Standing by the heap of *rust* were two old cars: one was a Morris Flatnose Cowley, circa 1932. The other was a Bullnose Morris with a hood top, but sadly this old car was missing its engine. I said to Winks, "Let's keep that old Bullnose," which was circa 1928. These old cars were starting to make good *loover*.

"No, Mike," Winks said, "it's got no engine or gearbox. It's no good. We will break it up for spares."

I will always remember that day. It was the day my mother's sister, Ada Gray, was buried. I never went to the funeral, because instead I was cutting up the old cars and scrap at Sutton. Just as I had finished cutting them up, old Fred Grimes came over and said,

"Why did you cut up that old Bullnose?"

I said, "it never had an engine."

"No," he said, "the engine for the Bullnose was in the old Morris Cowley."

I could have kicked myself! The spares off the Bullnose were sold to Peter Watts in Worstead for £10. Back then, the complete Bullnose was worth £200. You can't win them all, though it would be nice if you could.

Winks and I used to have all the batteries and scrap from Overstrand Garage. The garage was owned by a Mr Curtis, a very lovely *mush*. We called up there one day and this Mr Curtis asked if we could go down to the village and see an old retired army officer who had an old car that he wanted to dispose of. Off went Winks and I to the very large *kenner* (house). We rang the doorbell, and after a while the old *kooli* (soldier) appeared. He was a nice old *rye* (gentlemen), and he took us and opened up a large old garage. Inside was one of the nicest little *drags* I have seen. Winks and I took a look. It was a real beauty, like new, in mint condition...it shone like a *tanner* (shilling) on a sweep's arse. Winks took over and in his stuttering voice he said to the *guero* (man), "I will give to you a fiver for the old car." I started to walk out of the garage – I thought the old *mush* would kick off – but, believe it or not, he said, "Mr Lamb, I do not want that much. I will be very satisfied with four pounds." Christ, we had *monged* it. What a steal!

Let me tell you about the car. It was an early drophead coupé Lanchester saloon made by Daimler. It had a custom-made body and it was a classic. We went back to the garage to borrow a tow rope and also to thank Mr Curtis and slip him a *bar* (pound) for his help. Winks did not have a driving licence but he got behind the wheel and I started to tow him to North Walsham. Halfway home, a car cut us up and sharply pulled in front of us, and we had to stop. Winks started to *rap* (swear), "What the f**k are you doing? I nearly ran into you, you *minge*!" I managed to calm Winks down. The *mush* who had stopped us was a local *givengro* who we knew and who was a collector of old vehicles and carts. He wanted to buy our new *drag*. Knowing Winks, who would have sold it too cheaply, I stepped in and told the *gilly* (man) that it was not for sale.

At last we got it back to 'The Windy City'. I then set out to find a good buyer for it. I had already paid Winks for his share of the *jam-jar* (car). I wrote away to a firm in Buckinghamshire, and they were very interested in buying it...but another event occurred. On the day of my aunt Ada Gray's funeral (when as I told you I was away cutting up scrap over near Stalham), who should attend the funeral but Mike Kidd from Briston. Afterwards he had a word with my mother and said, "What have you got to sell me, Aunt Mary?" Winks was there and he said,

"Mike has a good old car." Mother said, "but I don't think he will want to sell it."

"Come on, Aunt Mary," urged the wily Mike Kidd. "Let me have a look at it."

He drove Mother down to ours and she showed him my *drag*. Anyway, what with Mother having a few too many stouts in her, she sold it (or gave it away) to Mike for £35. A nice bit of *loover* then, but nowhere near enough, considering what the car was worth. When I got home that night, I was well p****d off. I had just cut up an old Bullnose Morris which was worth £200 and sold it for spares for a tenner and then my mother had taken £35 for a car worth nearer £400. I had just not had a very good day! Did I need this? I would have to get back up that old *drom* tomorrow and start all over again. Who said this dealing is easy? It was not me!

*

While we are talking about Sutton near Stalham, I will tell you another little tale. I bet you can't wait to hear it. It is about old women. Christ, they craze you from the time you get up in the morning until the time you go to bed, but what would we do without them? Have a little peace, I should imagine. Like my old *mort*, they do your *kauns* (ears) in. They never stop *rokkering*. I suppose Adam was the first *mush* who had to put up with old Eve?

Back to Sutton, several years ago. I had to meet two old brothers who were *givengros*. They were giving up their farm at Sutton and they had a bit of *filth* (goods) to dispose of, hence me being on the scene. So I met up with them one night to have a bit of a deal or try to have a bit of a deal! When I got there these two old *gillys*, believe it or not, had their mouthy old *morts* with them. I knew they would upset the apple cart. At first, things were on track; they showed some nice old *covels* and me and the two old *givengros* were getting on like a house on fire. The old boys were real easy, so I thought to myself, "I'm going to have a nice little *touch* here." That was until the big mouth old *morts* started to put a spanner into the works. Every time the two old *gillys* agreed a price with me, the women stepped in. Christ, the stuff I bought was as dear as salmon. The old *gillys* could not get a word in edgewise with these two. To cut a long story short, when I left this quartet with the *filth* I had bought, I had earned *nicksas*. Those old women had worn me out. The Government ought to have hired them to get us out of Brexit... those two would have gotten us a good deal. They did not let their old *mushes* give anything away, bless them.

*

I used to regularly attend many sales and auctions years ago at Michaelmas time, during the autumn. Sometimes there could be as many as two or three farm auctions on in one day and if you could hit them right you could sometimes earn good *loover*. Most of us old Romany *chals* would go to buy a bit of *rust* and old farming bygones, as well as *gunners* (sacks). If there were only a few of you, you would have knock-out. What that means is one of us would buy all the *rust* so nobody else would be bidding. Then, after the sale was over, we would all stand in a ring or circle, always going clockwise, and take it in turns to put money on. Every time anyone dropped out, he would be paid out and the knock would continue until only one was left in. He would take the bought lots and share the money out with the persons left in. This knock only works well if you put your heads together and don't bid against one another. If you don't stand in, stuff in the sale makes too much and there is no room to make a profit.

Years ago, Mother and I went to a farm auction at Catton, Norwich. The entire farm was worked by horses and there was tons of *rust* there as well as rows and rows of old horse drawn farm gear, including a barn full of *gunners*. Also in the sale were two very large old farm *grais*. Mother and I were interested in the barn with the *gunners* in. Every dealing *mush* was at the sale. It was like Ali Baba and the Forty Thieves. As we were having a *dik* at the *gunners* in the barn, who should come over and see us but Mike Kidd from Briston? He said, "Leave them old sacks alone, Aunt Mary; we are going to have a knock-out and I am buying for the ring." Like a couple of *dinolos*, we let Mike *kin* the *covers*. We stood out, and Mike bought most of the stuff at the sale. After the sale was over, the Forty Thieves all got in the dark old *gran* (barn), and it was so dark in there all you could *dik* was the glow from the *tibloes* they were smoking. Anyway, Mike Kidd drew out from his *putsi* (pocket) the bill for the *covers* he had bought. Christ, it kicked off! He had also bought the two cart horses, plus other stuff no one wanted. They started shouting and swearing, suggesting we just knock the scrap and sacks out. "No," Mike said, "I bought the lot, so we will knock all of it out." No one wanted the old *grais* and other stuff. It got a little hot in that dark *gran*. There was so much *chingaripen* (arguing) someone nearly called in the *gavvers* (police). Mike had pulled a nice stroke but that day he got a lot of the old boys' backs up. Our feelings after that fiasco were that if you want something, don't stand in; buy it on your own back, win or lose – have a go. Plenty of those *mushes* would just go to a sale not to buy anything but to take part in the knock out, thus picking up easy *loover*.

*

Several years ago, over at Mautby near Great Yarmouth, I went to a farm sale. I can clearly remember who was there: Alfie Kidd from Holt...he was a nice old Romany *chal*, and John Wright from Erpingham, who was an old dealing boy, and myself. We were the only scrap dealers there; there was also one chap, a Docra from Yarmouth, but he did not hurt us! We bought a fair bit of *rust* for not too much *loover*. We knocked it out and I finished up taking it, plus we all had a nice bit of *vonger* (money). I paid Alfie and John out and the next day I went over to Mautby along with a *mush* who used to do a bit of *buty* (work) for me whose name was Jimmy Sizer. Also with me was a relation of mine who came from Yorkshire who was staying with us. He one day turned up out of the blue – Christ, was he a *dinolo*. His name was Johnie Lambert, a cousin of mine from Doncaster. He was not worth a tinker's cuss, but as we were keeping him in *scran* and *scimish*, I thought I might as well get a bit of *buty* out of him. Jimmy Sizer was also working for me at the time. He was cutting up the *rust* with an oxy cutter. The old matey from Doncaster was heaping it up, and I was carting it into Kings of Norwich on my old *moulder* .

All was going smoothly until Yorkshire Jack started to get on our nerves and disrupt things. He was being a prat, so I gave him a 16lb *demescro* (hammer) and told him to f***k off down the field and break up a little flat roll. Off he went and – what a *minge* – what did he do? He only went and broke up a set of Cambridge rib rolls that some old *givengro* had bought. He had paid almost £100 for them. "Oh my *dovel*, what have you done you w****r?" The only thing I could do was exchange the lot numbers on the two rolls and weigh in the rolls which prat face had broken up! We had to get the broken roll away before the farmer came looking for it. We loaded the broken roll up along with scrap. I was then about to drive off to Norwich when on the field came a little red tractor. I knew who it would be; yes, it was the old *givengro* who had bought the rolls. He started looking for his rolls, then over he came and saw his broken rolls on my *moulder*.

"You have broken and stolen my rolls!" he cried

"Your rolls? Where's the lot number?" I said.

He said, "You swapped them!"

Christ, we had a job with him. His old *boat* (face) went redder than his tractor. Good job there were three of us or I think he would have *coored* us – he was a big old *mush*.

The next day the auctioneer got in touch with me; he wasn't too happy. I had three choices, either find the *mush* another set of rolls (these might cost up to £150), pay him what he paid or go to Court and possibly be *stiffed* (arrested). I paid up! You see, it is not a good idea to be accompanied by *dinolos*. If you do, you pay the price. They also give you a bad name, and you don't need that.

I took Yorkshire Jack to North Walsham train station, paid for a one way ticket, gave him *desh bars* (ten pounds) and posted him back to Yorkshire. Let the old boys up there have him. If he had stayed any longer he would have bankrupt me!

*

Over at Bacton, about four miles from our place, lived a nice little *givengro*. My mother had several deals with him. We had to go to his *kair* (house) one day to buy a few scrap batteries off him. While we were in his garden Mother spotted a Victorian wire flower stand. It was *custi* (good). She said, "Do you want five shillings for that old stand?" The old *mush* grabbed her *loover* and said, "Whatever do you do with the old scrap? It don't weigh much at all." Anyway, this was years ago and we put it into Stalham sale and it made five pounds.

A few weeks later we were in Bacton again and the same old *mush* said to Mother,

"Mary, I have another piece of wire work, are you going to give me five shillings for it?"

"Yes," my mother said, and did, and we had another Victorian plant stand.

This one made six pounds in the sale. That should have been the end of that story but – hold you hard – it is not finished yet. The same old *gilly* got in touch with us.

"Mary," he said, "I have a large heap of scrap down at the farm. Being as you gave me a good price for them old wire stands, what are you going to give me for my heap of scrap?"

We took a good look at it. It was a nice bit of *rust* and Mother said, "I tell you what I am going to do, I am going to give you twenty pounds for it!" Christ, the old *chal* started to throw his covels (things) out of his pram. "What?" he cried, "twenty pounds for all that scrap? Why, you paid me five shillings for them old bits of wire. They was as light as pop. Now all this heavy stuff, you want to steal it!" We could not buy it. The old *gilly* thought we bought the wire stands for scrap, not Victorian garden antiques. Oh, well: you can't win them all. Silly old *mush*.

*

A long time ago, my Uncle Winks bought a large quantity of old *rust* off an old *massengro* (butcher) down at Bacton. Amongst the *rust* were a few old scrap cars. Winks never did have much *loover* so he *melled* (did not pay) the *mush*. He took all the best scrap away and told the old *massengro* he would pay him when he had carted it all away. The old *mush* kept on to Winks for his *loover*. Winks said, "I will pay you when I clear it all up," but he never did. This went on a long time. The old *mush* got sick and took Winks to court here at North Walsham to try and regain a little lost *vonger* (money). When Winks was summoned to the bench, the old *poknie* (magistrate) asked Winks,

"Mr Lamb, why have you not paid Mr _____ for the scrap

metal?"

"Because, Sir," Winks replied, "I told him when I cleared it all away then I would pay him."

The old *poknie* said, "Case dismissed. You are wasting my time and the Court's time. Mr Lamb has said he will pay when he moves the scrap. Damn, that is clear enough. You are dragging an honest man through the Courts."

Winks never did clear up the old car bodies and the old *massengro* never got *pestered*. You would not get away with a stunt like that today, but old Winks did!

Out On The Knocker

I think we have heard enough about the old scrap trade in this book. Let's move on, shall we? Move on to fresher ground. Christ, Reader, the things I do for you! It's still bloody hard writing all this stuff down. I ought to get myself a nice little secretary. Cor, that would not suit my old *mort*. She would *ding* (throw) me out and all my *covels* if I did. God bless her, although I still like the idea. What should we write now? I tell you what, Reader, I will take you on the *knocker* with me. If you watch me and listen you will see how I operate. You will then learn what it's like to go on the *knocker*. It's better than collecting old scrap. I will try and *kin* (buy) some nice bits of antique furniture and stuff, but being a true Romany if I do *dik* a nice bit of *rust* then I will still buy it! Let me put you in the frame and tell you what I will be doing. Yes it will be fun, why should it not be? All those lovely housewives and dolly-birds who we must persuade to part with their heirlooms.

It should be fun, but bear in mind we must be careful on the old *loover* front. Don't *bung* (pay) over the top. Remember we have to sell our *chats* (things) at the right price. The best stuff will go direct to local antique dealers. They sound posh! But don't you bloody believe it; give them half a chance and they will rob a workhouse child. Don't be put off by their smart, fancy suits or their glib tongues. They are much worse than hyenas, and they will take what they want and you, if you're not careful, will finish up just a pile of bones, because they will strip you bare. So, as you see, they are the enemy...but unfortunately we need to deal with them, so do not turn your back on them. Who said I don't like antique dealers?

We will also be dealing with another mob; these guys are known by the glorious name of 'Shippers'. Let's cut to the chase: they basically buy crap furniture, old jug and bowl toilet sets and all manner of *wafti* (bad) stuff. You, my friend, would not want it in your *kinder kair* (shithouse) but over that little piece of water, let me see, what's it called, the Atlantic Ocean? Yes, that's it: over there live some of our past relations. Oh yes, we used to be very friendly with them years ago, until they thought they would have a tea party and then they threw all our tea into the sea. That's why I reckon they only drink coffee now. But that was years gone by, and it now seems as though our long lost relations seem to like all this crappy furniture, so that's why guys like me sell to Shippers. It's much easier than taking it to the tip, plus you get paid for it. Can't be bad, dump it over there.

Reader, are you beginning to get the picture? Good *chats* we sell to antique dealers, and *kinder* to the Shippers. Then we have another range of goodies: good quality brass and copperware, nice desirable pieces, that our good folk over here desire. Just recently there has been a large influx of people from major cities moving down here to Norfolk, buying up nice old barns and houses and moving in amongst us. Some of them think they know the lot (and some of them do) but these folks need old brass candlesticks, copper kettles and ornaments to spruce up those old *grans* (barns). So, to supply them we did the local sales, but that was back then – not now. Everything has its day, and the days of local sales have gone. It's a great shame. For example, in the spot where old Jonathan Howlett had the Stalham sale, there now stands a dirty great supermarket. What's super about that? You tell me.

In years gone by, in medieval times, most towns in rural Norfolk had a market and they were all approximately a distance of seven miles away, a distance that one could comfortably walk. Let's press on, Reader! Are you starting to get an idea where I *blue* my *covels*? Come on, let's get up that old *tober* and *kin* (buy). Remember, when you buy antiques you have to buy at a price so you can sell them leaving a little meat on the bone. Remember my philosophy: buy today and sell tomorrow. Don't worry about the last shilling.

Today I am going to take you out to a few nice *kenner*s where I have bought in the past. Today I am taking you around Hanworth, Sustead and Aldborough. The first *kair* (house) I pull up to is a very small farmstead. The old *mush* here is half *custi*, and I have had a deal or two with him in the past. Up the garden path we go. Remember to always keep your *yoks* open – if you don't see things, you can't buy them!

Christ, I better watch out: I forgot this old *gilly* has got a *wafti juk* (bad dog). I remember the last time I was here, the bastard nearly had the arse out of my trousers! I can't see the *juk*. Good: he must be shut up! Even this trade on the knocker has its dangers. The old *gilly* is about – I can see him out in his back garden.

"Morning, Master," I shout. "How are you this lovely morning?"

He snarls at me, "What's lovely about it?"

"Why, Governor, it's a nice morning for me to spend a few pounds with you."

"A few pounds," he says, "the last time you were here, you gave me a little for that old school clock which I sold you. They tell me them old clocks are making over fifty pounds in Aylsham sale."

"Who told you that, Master?" Christ, I lost money on that old clock: I did not do any good with it. "Forget about the clock," I say, "let's see what you have got today."

"I don't think I have got anything for you today!"

He was a funny old *mush*: at the small farmstead he lived with his old *mort* but the old *mush* had another *rakla* living with him. It seems he had two *raklas*.

"You must have something I can buy?"

"Hang on a minute," he says, "I tell you what I have got."

"What's that, Master?" I ask.

"Well," he says, "up to about a year ago a syndicate from Ireland hired my shoot here along with my neighbour's shoot. Anyway, one of the women in the shoot used to shoot with a 28 bore gun. It was a 'Holland & Holland'. I always admired it and when the syndicate gave the shoot up, the lady gave me the gun. It's a lovely gun and I am getting too old to go shooting, so I might sell it to you."

Too old to go shooting? Not too old to have two wives? Some of them old Norfolk boys are a funny lot.

Inside the *kair* he goes and comes out with one of the best *yoggers* (guns) I have seen. It's in mint condition, a double barrel Holland & Holland of London, all nicely engraved. It's a star, plus the old *gilly* has almost a complete box of 28 bore cartridges for it. Then, like all Norfolk folk, he starts romancing the stone, telling me how, with this gun, he shot a crow about half a mile away. I have heard all this crap a dozen times. "It's not a bad little gun, Master," I say, "but it's a little on the small side. It's only a 28 bore, and most shooting folk prefer a 12 bore." It does not take me too long to prise the *yogger* from him for only fifteen pounds. I have a few more words with the old *chal* and leave him, along with his two wives. He's a brave old *mush* to have two wives! I have enough trouble and I have only got one. They do your head in, old women.

Anyhow, up the *drom* we go to the next little village of Sustead.

Let's see what we can find up there – it's only about a mile. As we drive slowly past a little old *kenner*, I *dik* an old *mush* looking at me through the *bor* (hedge), so I pull my old truck up and walk into his back garden. I then break the ice: that's to say I gain his confidence. A lot of these old boys are a little on the shy side and they are reserved. I think it's because they don't see many people down these little villages. You must not frighten them or you will not be able to buy anything.

"Hello, Governor, how are you doing? Blast, you have got some good spuds in that old garden of yours!"

The old *mush* starts to warm to me, and if I play it right I reckon I could *mong* a few of these *puvengros* (spuds). Back to business.

"What have you got for me today...anything in your old shed over there?"

I can see he has a large old brick shed. It might be hiding something in there for me. The secret when dealing with these old country boys is to lead the way: start walking towards the shed, and he will follow. Be bold and try and spot something. Anyway, the old boy opens the shed door and we draw in. I have a quick *dik* around. On the wall hangs a *custi* old pair of coach lamps. They would be worth about 25 *bars*. There is also a bit or two of old horse harness, which always sell if they have a few brasses on them, as these have.

I place the lamps on the ground and have another glance into the shed, spotting a nice old Victorian lamp table. Another 25 *bars*. I place this with the other *covels*, look the old mush in the *yoks* and I say, "Here you go Master. I am going to give you a tenner to take this old gear out of your way: it is cluttering up your shed!" The *gilly's* mouth drops, and I can see he expected more. I take a ten pound note from my long melford[1] and give

---
1 A cloth bag to hold money

it to the *mush*. He never says a word. I pick up my *covels* and go out to the truck. The old *mush* never takes his *yoks* off of me! I think he is a little *thrashed* (frightened) of me, but I don't know why. I am harmless enough. Things are going sweet this morning, but will it last? I hope so.

At the next few *kenner*s, I do not do any good. One old *rakla* was watching me from behind her curtains, because she thought I was going to *chore* something. Another young *rakla* was, I think, a bit short of *loover*, and she would have sold me anything but the poor *juva* (girl) never had anything any good. Also, she was getting a little flirty with me. She had on one of those tiny miniskirts and she was bending over, and I could see next week's washing! You have to be careful with some of these *monistas* (women). You could have some big old *mush* after you! I don't need all this agro. Another thing when out on the knocker: when you are going up people's garden paths or going around the back of a *kair*, let the person know you are coming by whistling or humming a tune. Plenty's the time I have *jelled* (gone) round the back of a *kair* and there has been a *rakla* sunning herself with her *tootchis* (breasts) hanging there in the morning sun!

*

On another occasion, on Hanworth Common, my mother had knocked on a *stigur* (door) and on the step was a pile of old car batteries with two suitcases stood beside them. Out of the house came a smart young *moll* (woman).

"Do you want to sell them old car batteries?" Mother asked

"No," she cried, "they belong to my old man and I am now leaving him! I am waiting for my boyfriend."

At that moment a truck pulled up; it was the *rakla's* new *mush* who I recognised as Micky Thurston. He was a lovely *fly* old boy. Off went Micky and his *rakla* to start a new life together. I think things went well for them and they were together many years, God bless them. We never bought the old batteries, and the *mush* must have wondered where his *mort* had gone. I have seen some funny old things when I was on the knocker.

*

Christ, I don't know about you, but my old *curlo* (throat) is getting a bit on the dry side. It's all this *rokkering* with these old *Gorgios*. I'll tell you what we will do: it's only two miles to Aldborough Green, where we can have *shant* in the Black Boys. Seeing as I am taking you with me for a ride and teaching you all the tricks of the trade, I think you should get the *scimish* in. Sorry, I was only joking – I will buy you one. There are two *kitchemas* on the green, and the other one is the Red Lion. Christ, I know it's a Monday, but there is not a soul in the *kitchema*. In we go. The old landlady is serving; she looks an old *juk*, but – I tell you something – I would not like to get on the wrong side of her. Christ, she's a size. I would rather keep her a week than a fortnight. "Good morning, Madam," I say. I can tell at once that she doesn't like Romanies. A lot of these village pubs have had trouble in the past what with there being a large fair here every year. I order two pints, one for me and one for my reader. I give her a 'John Bradbury' and say, "Take one for yourself." That seems to change her. She says she will have it later and she takes money for a drink for herself from my *loover*.

She has a few horse brasses hanging on the wall, so I ask, "Will you buy a few more horse brasses to go with those? I have just bought some down the road at Sustead. They are nice brasses on their leather straps. Can I sell you them?"

She says, "My old man is not here, and I leave all the buying to him."

I think, this is not going anywhere! So I start to finish my *shant*. Through the *glazer* (window) I can see old Tom Wright on the green. He's a nice old boy. He gets into a few *kairs* on the green doing odd jobs and sometimes he picks up a few things. I finish my *shant* and walk out, bidding the old *beng* (devil) a good day. She glares at me and I walk out over to have a word with Tom.

Unfortunately, he never had anything, so let's get back into my old truck and go to a *kenner* (house) on the bottom of the green. It's nearly dinner time and the old *mush* I am going to see is the local postman, old Herbert Knights. Christ, I have bought some stuff off him over the years. Herbert, being a postman, starts early and finishes early, so he has a fair bit of time on his hands. When Herbert finishes his round, he does odd jobs in old folks' *kairs*: painting, DIY, etc. Now, some of these people have not got much *loover* – they are like me! So, Herbert, instead of taking money, will sometimes take goods such as little pieces of antiques. Now, this is where I come in. Fairly regularly I will call on old Herbert and buy some nice *covels* from him. That's why I am at his gate now; I want to catch him before he goes off doing his DIY rounds.

"Hello, Mr Knights," I say. Never call anyone older than yourself by their first name: have respect.

"Hello, young Harmer," he replies. "What are you after?"

"You know me, if I can earn a crust that will suit me fine."

Herbert lights his *tibloe*. He always smokes with a cigarette holder. Herbert is one of those old Norfolk boys who you will never see again...salt of the earth.

"I have something that may interest you, I have had it under my old workbench for years! Come into my workshop and I will hike it out." he says.

From under a bench Herbert pulls out a large flat rosewood box. It's smothered in brass. Herbert places it on the bench and opens the lid. It's a beauty. Inside the box are various shaped compartments and on the lid on the inside is a trade label with – would you believe this – the name 'Joseph Manton, London'. Cor, that gets my old ticker (heart) a-going. Manton of London was one of the best gun makers in the country.

"Pity the gun is not in the case." says I to Herbert.

"I had the gun which went in it."

"You did? Where is it now?"

"I sold it. It was an old muzzle-loading fowling gun. The person I sold it to did not want the case."

Christ! Back then, the gun and case would have been worth over two hundred pounds. It seems there are still *dinolos* about. I buy Herbert's gun case for a fiver and next day drop it into an antique shop for £50. Not a bad day's work, but if only I had the gun, too.

Stalham Sale

Right, Reader, now you will have to get out of my old truck. Like I say, Romany folk do not work in the afternoons, if they can help it! I have taken you for a ride, I bought you a *shant* and I have, I hope, taught you about the knocker – so now go back to your humble abode. Tomorrow, I will, if you can get round mine soon enough, take you back in time to the Stalham sale. In my opinion, I would say Stalham sale was the best one in Norfolk. It took bit of beating! There I will show you some nice old dealing boys and let you in on how I operate. See you tomorrow. Don't you be late or I will leave without you. When you do the sales you must never be late; remember the early bird.

Stalham sale is every Tuesday, come rain or shine. The auctioneers are Jonathan Howlett. This old sale had been going since medieval times but, alas, it is no more. Greed has crept in – money talks. A large supermarket now occupies what was once the old sale ground. Another thing that helped the demise of the sales was the auctioneers themselves. They kept upping their commissions until they were better off than the vendor. So today most selling is done on Ebay and other internet sites.

Christ, look at the time: if we don't get there early we might as well have kept at home. Never be late! Stalham is only 8 miles from North Walsham, walking distance. If it's summertime and the weather is good, you display your *covels* outside. At Stalham sale one man has top billing, and that's old Jack Cleveland from Lowestoft. He brings large amounts of stuff in every week, and he almost runs the sale. He has top pitch. His stuff is always sold first. He's a top man! Then we, the smaller fry, have our pitches. The idea is, it's a big sale so you want your stuff sold before it gets too late and punters are beginning to go home. My mother and I have been selling good quality brass and copperware and bric-a-brac for years. As Stalham is on the edge of the broad, it attracts a lot of holiday makers, who like to take home a few items bought from the sale. Trade antique buyers as well will check the sale out to see what's on offer.

My mother and I take it in turns to watch and mind the pitch. This is important in order to see who is interested in your stuff. Also, trade buyers will leave prices with buyers, so sometimes you can hear what prices they have left. Another thing is you do not put reserves on your gear; instead, you watch the punters who are bidding and run your stuff up as far as you can without buying it back yourself. Enough of this drivel; let me tell you roughly what I have got in the sale today: firstly, a nice pair of coach lamps which I have shined up, the pair I bought off that old *mush* at Sustead. There's also the old harness with the brasses on and his Victorian oil lamp. All my goods will be shining like a *shohorry* (shilling) on a sweep's *chad* (arse). Plus, I have a few more *chats* (things) on my pitch.

It's a nice day, but I think it will be a scorcher. Mother is minding the pitch, so I will go and get a cup of *peava* (tea) and a bit of *scran*. There's a nice tea hut on the sale ground, run by Harold Ward and his wife from Trimingham near Cromer. In I go, and sitting in the corner is old Brewster from Saxthorpe. Brewster, like me, comes every week. He buys mostly large pieces of old furniture and also old silver pocket watches which he sells to American Air Force guys based at Sculthorpe Airfield (which is out Brewster's way).

"How you doing?" I ask Brewster.

"Not too bad, Mike," he replies. I buy him a cup of *peava*. He's not a bad old boy.

Next to roll onto the saleground are Ray and Doreen Wright from North Walsham. They are always late! Doreen has a small bric-a-brac *shobi* (shop) in Walsham. Ray, her *rom* has a fruit and veg round. They are a nice couple. Old Peter Watts from Worstead is here. Peter sometimes puts a few lots into the sale but he often buys old motor car artefacts. His father is old Alec Watts from Worstead. He was known as Tailor Watts. Romanies would go to him to have their special Romany suits made at £2.10s a pop, which was good money then. They still keep coming, and the old sale ground is filling up quick. There's Mad Harry from out Yarmouth way, whose real name is Ray Knights. He's a good operator; I have seen him selling cheap *tomfoolery* (jewellery) out of a suitcase.

Two of old Tighty Hatch's boys are here. Dennis Hatch is now a top antique buyer of some repute. He won't see anything being given away today. His older brother, Freddy Hatch, is also here. What a character – he's the black sheep of the family and is sometimes looked down on by his brothers, but I like Freddy. By the way, Freddy had more *raklas* than Warren Beatty. He's a legend. Who else is here? Dick Foster and his son from Norwich, they will be selling flowers, shrubs, etc. They're nice old *chals*.

Coming onto the sale ground late is Manny Waterfield and his niece Collena, driving a large old *moulder*. They have got half a load of *rust* on it. Manny and Collena won't be buying too much stuff, as their first port of call will be the Maids Head, right next to the sale ground. When they come out of there they will be as *motty* as two juks. The sale ground is alive with folks: it's heaving with bodies. It should be a good day – I hope so! What's that noise? It's little old Sam Bean from Sutton, ringing the auctioneer's bell, summoning us for the start of the sale. Out comes Paddy Ling, who is a fine auctioneer. He's quick, he's smart and he doesn't contemplate fools or time wasters. He has about 600 lots to sell today. With him is the sale porter, Ted Lawrence, who will show the lots off. Jack Cleveland's goods will be sold first, he's a top man!

After a while, Paddy Ling reaches our lots, and it's a good sale.

The old pair of coach lamps sell well, as does the Victorian table lamp. All in all, we have a tidy *touch* (result). A few bits we got back, so I put them away on my truck, wait a little while, then go and draw out some *vonger* (money). Then, like most Romanies, we head for the *ginger beer shop*, The Maids Head, for a few *jam jars*.

Who is in here today? Old Manny and Collena are here, because they are always here. Manny looks well *motty*. Collena is roaring with laughter. She's a strong *rakla* and she gives an old *clod hopper* (farm worker) an almighty slap on his back. Christ, she nearly knocks him on to the floor, but it's all good fun! Later, Collena will have to drive her lorry home with Manny. It's getting nice and lively in here now. Who is that over the back of the *livnoker* (pub)? It's Sidney and Mike Kidd, father and son from Briston. Sidney buys me a bottle and we have a yarn. Sidney and Mike are what are known as pub operators. They get in a *kitchema* and then they start to work. They buy an old boy a drink and learn from him about where things are or what he has got for sale, thus getting a living from the comfort of the *livnoker*. I tell Sid and Mike about an old *Gorgio* who has a set or two of good driving harnesses which they may be able to buy on the way home. I tell them I will show them when we finish drinking, which will not be too soon because at the moment the old *scimish* is flowing. My cup runs over. The place is packed, and most are spending what they have just earned. It's a good job we have had a good day! It's getting to be 3 o'clock and some folks are beginning to head home, but some still have a little *loover* left in their *putsis*.

You see, Reader, when this took place there were no breathalyzers. If you got in your *jam jar* (car), you could drive it as long as you didn't run over anyone and *muller* them! We wait for Sidney and Mike to follow us. We are taking them to Worstead New Inn. It's a *kitchema* in a small village about 5 miles down the *drom* near North Walsham.

At last we get there. The nice old landlady knows us, and she should do, as we have spent a nice bit of *vonger* with her in the past. The *kitchema* is closed but she opens up and lets us in for more *scimish*. My God it tastes good; the more you have the more you want! While my mother is drinking I take Mike outside to meet this nice old Norfolk *chal*. It's old Bob Spanton, who runs a cattle float business taking animals to local markets. Also, old Bob likes his *grais* and I know he has got two good sets of *straps* (harnesses). Mike and I have a word with Bob. Bob lives next door to the pub; how handy is that?

Tighty Hatch (back to camera) with a bunch of kids back long before social distancing and masks. Do you remember those days, readers?

Mike soon has a deal. He buys two sets of brown Moroccan harnesses, slips me a *desh* (ten) 'John Bradburys' and the day is getting a little better. Mike puts the *straps* on to his truck and, like most Romanies, he must take something home to his *chavies* and *mort*. Mike says, "Come with me, I want a bit of *mass* (meat)."Just opposite the New Inn is a *massengros* (butchers). The butcher is George Norgate. In we walk, and Mike has a yarn with George and says, "I want a piece of your best fillet steak." George cuts Mike a large piece and Mike *bungs* (pays) him. We then draw back and have a few more *jars* and then it's time to hit the *tober*. Christ, what a good day it has been. You see, Reader, Romanies always try to put two days into one – live in the moment, earn a bit of *loover* and meet up with other Romanies and get *motty* together. What a good life!

Where's Manny and Collena? They are still in Stalham. Christ, those two will be in a state when they get home! God bless them and now, Reader, I must ask you to return to your *kair*, if you have one! You have been with me to Stalham sale: savour the moment, because it will never ever happen again. It's all ended... no more Stalham sales. How very sad. I will let you know if I want you with me anymore! By the way, you tight-fisted *juk*, you never bought me a *shant*. You are a typical *Gorgio* (non-Romany), tight as a drum.

A few pages back in this book, I told you about the Holland & Holland 28 bore which I half *monged* (begged) off old Barker at Sustead. I sold the gun to a private collector of guns, Leslie Curtis who owned Overstrand Garage. He was the nice *mush* who put me and Winks onto the old Lancaster car at Overstrand. Sadly, Mr Curtis has passed away, but I think his family still run the garage. They most probably still have the old gun! You must have seen by reading this book how most deals are done: we dealers gather little snippets of information which leads us to a deal. Always asking and probing, that is how most stuff is sourced and found. Also, any tip-off is always rewarded with a drink and a bit of *loover* placed in your *vast* (hand). Most entrepreneurs and up-market businessmen will have dinner lunches to seek and discuss business, and Romanies will have a business lunch in a pub. This will consist of a cheese roll and a *shant*. That's how we do it – that way you do not need a smart Saville Row suit, unless some old *Gorgio* has thrown one away!

Bonney Price (left) with Mike Harmer in front of the 'trailer-vardo' at the Marshgate workshop in Spa Common.

Bonney Price

Right, Reader, talking about this tripe has started to get on my nerves, so let's find something else to chat about. After all, the heart of this *lil* (book) are the Romanies, and that's the reason I am writing it: also because all of you want to hear about these mysterious people, don't you? I tell you what, I will be glad when I have finished all this *porengripen* (writing), because my old *vangus* (fingers) are aching. This trouble is, I told you so many tales about them in my first book, I keep running out of tales to tell of the past. Maybe I better move onto more recent times..

O dordi (oh dear), here we go. I have mentioned him before, but there is this old Romany friend of mine, Bonney Price, whose father was old Crimea Price. Most Prices are called Posh Price, from the Romany word *posh* which means 'half'. So they were known as Half Prices. I first met Bonney when he and his family used to *hatch* on the old common down here where I live. Bonney's dad has some good coloured *grais* and some good Bill Wright bowtop wagons. To own a Bill Wright was like owning a Rolls Royce of wagons. Bill Wright made his *vardoes* at Haigh in Yorkshire. You would be hard pressed to find a better wagon.

You might say that Bonney Price and I grew up together. Every summer when the Prices came onto the common, Bonney would seek me out. When we were old enough we would go out with my old 410 *yogger* and shoot a bit of game, like a few rabbits. When we got a little bit older, Bonney Price and I would go into many of the old dumps around here. We would pick up a good lot of *smut* (brass) and *lollo* (copper), etc. Then, strangely, I never saw Bonney for a few years, until one day – like all Romanies do – he just turned up. He had got himself a lovely Romany *mort* and a *chavie*. He had got *rommed* and he had a nice little Bedford *moulder* and a *custi trailer* (good caravan).

Bonnie would again come onto the common every year and come and see me! He still does, even though he is now 78 years old and has at last sadly moved into bricks. That's to say he now lives in a bungalow, much against his wishes, but he's not too well at the moment. He has had a severe heart attack and a bad stroke which has sadly robbed him of his speech, so poor old Bonney cannot *rokker* anymore. He also cannot read or write, which has left him in a bad way, but he is still going. At the time I am writing this book, my sons and I are making Bonney a bow top wagon on a modern car trailer. You see, with old Romany *chals* old habits die slowly. So, Reader, if you should see a brightly painted bow top going up the M25 at 70mph, it will be Bonney. If it is Bonney, take your *titfa* (hat) off, if you wear one, and tell yourself that you have just seen a legend. Hang in there, Bonney!

Just before we let old Bonney go, let me tell you a tale about him. Bonney told me when he had his heart attack and he was close to *mullered*, his *mort* and family never came near him when he was bad in the *naflinken* (hospital). When Bonney recovered, he turned his back on them. One day he was enjoying a bit of *smoothing* (fishing) beside a lovely lake when his *mort* kept calling him on his mobile phone. Bonney had had enough, so he said, "Go away, woman, and talk to the fish." With that, Bonney threw his mobile into the middle of the lake. She was not around when poor old Bonney needed her.

LIFE ON THE DROM

Come on, Reader, I tell you what we will do. Let's turn the clock back, let's say to the early 19th Century. I will take you around some of these nice old commons and green lanes. We will be travelling with my old grandfather, Butty Lamb, and his *mort*, Mary-Ann. Have you ever heard a sweeter name? Mary-Ann. My old grandmother is not as sweet as her *nav* (name) implies, however. She was brought up in the true Romany way, where women were as hardy as the men. All had large families, and Mary-Ann had fourteen *chavies*, bringing up twelve. Imagine looking after a family of that size, living in a wagon that's about 10ft by 6ft. Plus, each day she would have to walk, some days 20 miles, *calling* (selling) her *tograms* and *mushes*. When her long day had ended, she would have to *scran* (feed) everyone, and also make and get *covels* ready for another day's *calling*. I think a lot of *Gorgios* over the years have romanced and put the Romanies in an idyllic situation, portraying a life of pure unreal bliss. You could not get further from the truth. Life on the *drom* was anything but idyllic. It could be said that at times it was best described as totally horrendous.

Back to old Butty Lamb. Let's have a look at the world from his point of view. Bear with me, Readers, while I strap on his boots and see the world through his eyes. Right, off we go. Look at me. I'm in the prime of life with only ten *chavies* - there will be another two by the time I'm done. A day ago we set up camp (or *hatching*, as we call it) between ourselves on South Creake Common, near Fakenham. Nestled nearby is a family of Brinkleys, close relations of mine. Over yonder there are some of old Baggy Brown's brothers with their kin and further afield are the Boswells from Lincolnshire - their descendants have a fine Romany museum in Lincolnshire.

Now, at South Creake common, you can sometimes go a week

or more before the *gavvers* (police) move you on. There is no let up from this constant harassment; we are Romanies and no one wants us on their doorstep. Perhaps the day will come one of these days when we will be allowed to live our lives the way we wish to, but not now. It's getting harder to *mong* a pail of *pani*. We are looked down upon and pushed from one old common to another. A few others and I have nearly had enough, because you can only be pushed so far. He's also heard that some Romanies are beginning to settle down into bricks, move into *kenner*s, buy a bit of *puv*, pull their old wagons on and leave the *tober*. How sad, but maybe with all my *chavies*, I should be considering it. It's getting much harder every day, as they keep pushing us from our commons and green lanes.

For the next few days, Mary-Ann and I try to relax and go out *kettering costies* (gathering wood) for *tograms*. Linen pegs help you to survive. You will never get rich making them, but the whole family will help to make them. On a good day we can turn out about six gross. There are 144 pegs in a gross so that would be in the region of 864 pegs. We also *fake a mush* (mend an umbrella) or two, as there's more *loover* in *mushes* (umbrellas). Most of my *loover* is earned by my dealing in some *custi grais*. I *blue* the coloured ones to other *needis* (travellers). *Gorgios* don't like coloured *grais*, so I breed some bay or chestnut. I *blue* them mostly to *Gorgio* tradesmen. I *blued* one a fortnight ago to a *mush* who runs a carrier business. He only wants *custi* bits of blood. I sold him my best bay colt, which I broke in for 70 *bars* (pounds), a nice bit of *vonger*. Tomorrow I am off to see a *mush* who I hear is looking for a good sort of *grai*. He keeps a *kitchema* at Docking, which is only about three miles up the *tober*. We will *jell* off this common in the morning with my *vardoes* and then head for Grimston common near Kings Lynn, stop at Docking on the way and I will see if I can fence my *tit* (mare) to the *holeno* (landlord).

Before I *jell* tomorrow I must have a new set of *petuls*

(horseshoes) put on the *tit*. This afternoon I will take it up to North Creake, where there is an old *coroengro* (blacksmith) that might shoe my *tit*, depending on what sort of mind he is in. You see, no one likes us and he will not be too keen to shoe my *tit* if I don't throw him a little extra *loover*. Sometimes when I have been here before, I have had to buy him a stone flagon of *scimish* from the Jolly Farmers before he would think about shoeing my *tit*. I tell you – I am thinking of packing this all in, settling down, leaving the travelling to the younger ones, because this life has had it.

After much moaning, the *coroengro* puts me a good set of *petuls* on my *tit*, and I ride her back to my *hatching tan* (stopping place). It's getting a bit late now, and it will soon be dinner time. I can *dik* that old Baggy Brown is still *soving* (sleeping). I think last *rarti* (night) old Baggy went down to the Ostrich Pub and got too much *scimish* down his neck. I see my *mort* has caught and put away my game cocks, and she has also put my best cob in the *sharps* (shafts) of my wagon. She and the *chavies* have also loaded up most of our *covels* onto the Lambeth trolley, so we are nearly ready to *jell*. Mary-Ann has also put the *yog* out and raked away the ashes to leave a tidy site: some of these other *needis* leave a *hindity* (dirty) site. This earns us a bad name.

After about a half hour we are off and there's nothing like it, brother, getting on that old *tober*. This is what freedom is all about. Eight miles to Docking, and the *tit* with her new *petuls* is tied beside my big coloured *grai* and she looks very *custi*. A *grai* when it has just been shod goes so much better, like us when we get a new pair of *chokkers* (shoes). I am glad to get off Creake common; the place is good...it's just the *mushes* on it. I don't get on very well with Baggy Brown and I don't think he is in love with me! We got wrong with one another about two years ago – where was it? I know! It was on Crosswight common near North Walsham. We had a bit of a *coorapen* (fight) over an old *grai*. All *coorapens* are over *grais* or *raklas*. We had a fair go! I won and we shook hands, as all Romanies do after a *chingaro* (fight), but old Baggy has never forgotten it. Some folk don't seem to move on, and that's why lately I keep thinking I should *kin* a bit of a *puv*, pull my old *vardoes* on and pack it in. I have also noticed lately that some of my pals and relations are getting all high and mighty, falling out with one another as *needis* have been earning good *loover*. I think it is a good thing. *Loover* can change folks. My *dovel*, I hope Romanies don't go down the same *drom* as *Gorgios* or we will be finished. We must, if we are to survive, stick together and put all this aside.

It's a glorious day in old England's green lanes. It's spring as my old cob draws us on to Docking. I can hear the lovely echo of the cuckoo...a sweeter sound you will never hear! He is telling us that spring is here, so let's rejoice like the cuckoo and enjoy this fine spring morning. After about an hour and a half we arrive at Docking, where nobody rushes out to greet us. In the middle of Docking is a large old public well where we stop and draw up a pail of *pani* for ourselves. We try to get some for the *grais* but these *Gorgios* will not let us have any for the *grais*. Christ, they are *juks*. This village is known as 'Dry Docking', because water here is scarce. When you lower your pail down the well it is ages before it hits water. It's chalk country here and the *pani* is deep! We get a drop for ourselves and I rub a wet cloth over the *grais'* mouths to refresh them. I have to see the old holeno *mush* who wants a *grai* and I will get some *pani* off him, hopefully. They resent us the locals here; mind you, that's their problem.

I manage to track down the holeno *mush*. He's a mush who loves horses. He also takes to me and we start to deal. First, I take the freshly shod *tit* from the wagon *sharps* (shafts). He, being a horse man, can see that my *tit* is wearing a new set of *petuls* and I can tell he likes what he sees. I get my son Lazarus to put the *grai* through her paces, and can't that *chavo* ride a grai! Up and down Docking High Street he goes. An old *monista* (woman) nearly gets knocked over. You ought to have heard her! "You flaming gyppos!" she screams like a banshee. My son roars with laughter – what an old *beng* (devil). As the folks around here are getting a little upset, I tell Lazarus that's enough. The carrier I can see likes the *tit* so I ask 80 *bars* for her. I know this is too much, but as the mush is a dealing man, I know he will try and knock me down and he does. He steps up to me, grasps my hand, holds his other hand up ready to smack mine and says,

"I will give you 50 pounds which is about right for a horse of this class."

"I can't take that, *mush*." I cry. I am old Butty Lamb and I still have a little dealing left in me. "Why, I paid more than that for it. It's a nice little mare. On my poor old dead mother's grave, would I lie to you?" I think I have him.

"How about 60 pounds?" he says. This time a little keener.

"Well, I tell you what, because I like you, brother, I will take 65 pounds." If my dear wife Mary-Ann knew I was giving this little mare away she would leave me and I would have to bring all my *chavies* up on my own: *o dordi*. He slaps my hand – we have a deal. I am happy and the *mush* is happy, and he lets us fill our cans up with his *pani*. We both go into his *kitchema* nearby to seal the deal and he pays me out in *sonneco* (gold sovereigns). After all the hassle of the last few days, it is good to meet a nice true *rye* (gentleman) and be taken into the *kitchema* and bought a *shant*. Many's the time when we were refused a drink in the *kitchemas*.

Right now I am feeling good; I have *loover* in my *putsi* (pocket). I will soon hear the sound of *bowlers* (wheels) on the *tober*, a sound a *Gorgio* will seldom hear. I shake hands and say farewell to the holeno. We won't get to Grimston common today, what with *blueing* the mare and *scimishing* in the *kitchema*. The time is getting on. Mary-Ann and the *chavs* have been into some *shobis* (shops) and bought some *scran*. I think, because it's getting a little late, I will *hatch* on Fulmodeston common for the *rarde* (night). Being in a good frame of mind, it would be *custi* to meet up with some other Romany *chals*. With this life you never know what is around the next bend! Also, you never know who you will meet. It's not long before my cob gets us over to Fulmodeston. It's good – I can see *tuv* (smoke) coming from one or two *yogs*, and I can see a rough old kite wagon in need of a little paint! It's old Charlie Gaskin. What a lovely old chal. He's got a large family; I don't recall how many *chavies* he has, but he must have enough to half fill that old school down the *tober*. Charlie might have a *wafti* (bad) old *vardo* but he always has some good *tits* and I reckon tonight after old Charlie has had a few *shants* – he always draws down to the local kitchema – I will then try and kin (buy) one of his nice grais (horses).

There's another family *hatching* here, but I don't think I know them and they look a *chori* (poor) lot. Their old *grais* look washed out. In all, the whole family look like they have had a bad time. Later on, I will go and visit them. It's customary in our Romany circle when meeting a stranger on a *hatching tan* (stopping place) to wait until that family has *scranned* (eaten). It's good manners to take the family a small gift as well. Even though we are stopping on an old rough common, it's important to put one's best *togs* on. Your *mort* wears her best *covels* and you leave any *chavies* at your *vardo*. Folks who you are visiting will get their best china *dui and dass* (cups and saucers) out. And you only sit around someone's *yog* if you are invited. So you see, Reader, we Romanies are not as primitive as you thought.

Although the common does not belong to anyone, when you are *hatching* on the common around your *yog* and *vardo*, it's yours and other Romanies will most certainly respect it. While the commons don't belong to anybody now, who knows? In the years ahead, I can see us Romanies losing the right to *hatch* there and that will be a very sad and dismal day. Christ, what am

I moaning on about? I am a proud old Romany *chal*. Tonight I will go and see old Charlie Gaskin and see if I can *kin* that nice little roan *tit* off him which I had a *dik* at, but old Charlie will not be back from the *kitchema* until a little later! So Mary-Ann and I will *jell* to the other family who I don't know. Mary-Ann has found a nice pair of *duis* (cups) and they are very *rinkeni* (pretty), just like my old *mort*! If Mary-Ann hears me I will have a frying pan on my *shero* (head). We have *scranned* our *chavies* and ourselves. I will tend the *grais* later. There's not too much *chaw* (grass) on this old common. It's had several Romanies *hatching* on it lately.

Mary-Ann and I draw over to the Romanies who I don't know. There is a headman and his *mort* and about eight *chavies*, but these *chavies* are well mannered and the *mush* tells them to *jell* and they disappear into the *rarde*. We get invited to their *yog* and, my *duvel*, they look *chori* (poor). The mush is about fifty years old, but his *mort* is much younger, hence all these *chavies*. We shake *vasts* and make ourselves known. I say to them, "I am Butty Lamb and this here is my *mort*, Mary-Ann." The *mush* bids us to be seated which we do in Romany style: I sit cross legged and Mary-Ann sits on the *puv* (ground) with her legs tucked under her. Mary-Ann gives the *chori rakla* the pair of *duis* and she is well pleased with them. "How far have you come?" I ask the *mush*. He's smoking a short, broken stem *swegler* (pipe) and lights it with a piece of hot *cosh* from the *yog*.

"Well pal," he says, "we have come all the way from North Yorkshire and we have been pushed off every bit of *puv* we have *hatched* on. So, you see, pal, we have not had enough time to earn a bit of *loover*. My *grais* are like ourselves, worn out."

"Well," I say, "...brother, you have been through a hard time, You will be alright here for a week or more to sort yourself out, rest them *grais*, and get earning yourself some *loover*. I will tell you where around these parts you can *hatch*. I know what it's like travelling in a strange county." This seemed to cheer the *mush* up.

Mary-Ann and I *rokker* with them for about an hour, then we wish them a good *rardi* and draw over to old Charlie's *yog*. Charlie has been back for almost an hour. He has *scranned*. His old *mort* Charlotte beckons us over to their *yog*. She's a lovely old dear who's got one of these faces that looks like it's been lived in, with sharp black *yoks*. She has more wrinkles on her *mui* (face) than I have got hair on my head.

"Where have you been travelling Butty?" the old *mort* says.

"Not too far, Charlotte," I say, "just round these old commons in these parts but I'm heading up to Grimston common. I hear that some of my 'lations are *hatching* up there."

Old Charlotte keeps poking the *yog*, causing the *tova* (smoke) to go over our best bits of *togs*.

"Stop that," cries old Charlie, "...you know what they say, if you poke the fire, you will get *cambori* (pregnant)." Christ, old Charlotte let out!

"You old *minge*, get *cambori*? I am too old for all that stuff. By the way, you old *juk*, you haven't made the old wagon rock for years, so you won't get anyone *cambori*!"

We all roar with laughter. There's nothing better than seeing two old Romanies stirring one another up!

"I tell you what, Butty, come and see me in the morning – not too early as I have got to look after old Charlotte –"

"Why, you old *minge*, you could not look after an old *kani* (chicken)!" Old Charlotte gives me a sly wink.

"I will try and *blue* you a nice little *grai* which might suit you" continues Charlie.

"Nice little *grai*, Charlie? You never had a nice little *grai* in your life!"

"You monkey's *minge!*" he cries. "On my poor old dead mother's life, it's the best little hoss in bloody Norfolk."

"It's getting late, Charlie, I will see you in the morning. *Custi rarde.*"

Laughing to ourselves as we draw back to our own *vardo*, Mary-Ann says to me,

"You have not rocked the *vardo* lately."

"No," I said. "I won't be, either."

I am up early next morning. I want to have a deal with Charlie, as I am getting a bit low on *grais* which I want to *blue* but I don't want to hang around this old common much longer. I want to meet up on Grimston common with some of my 'lations, the Gray family who I have not seen for about nine months. Last time I think it was at Ingham Fair near Stalham. I have already got the *yog* going and cooked Mary-Ann and the *chavies* a bit of *scran*. All Romanies like to *scran* early because you never know when you will get your next bit of *chor* (food). Hopefully it will be on Grimston common.

"Are you about, Charlie?" I cry. After a while, Charlie opens his *vardo* door, and he does not look too bright.

"You don't look too good, Charlie. What, did old Charlotte keep you up? I thought I heard that old wagon shaking."

"F**k you, Butty. I told you last night, I am past all that!"

"That's what you tell me, Charlie!" Cor, he is savage:

"If I were a little younger I would *coor* you."

"Would you now, Charlie? If you were younger, you'd still be in that old wagon with Charlotte."

In my *vast* I have a *duis of peava* (cup of tea) for Charlie, since I do not want to wait until he lights his *yog*.

"Come on, Charlie, drink that *peava* up, and let's see this broken winded *grai* you've got."

"Broken winded? It's the best little *tit* in Norfolk."

Charlie has not put it in the farmer's field like I have. I got mine out of the *puv* early. Charlie has his staked out on chains across the common. We draw over and they are a good bunch of *grais*. I spot a nice, young coloured *tit* which I like. It is half broken in; I have seen it walking beside his wagon and I know it is a good 'un.

"How cheap is that little *tit*?" I ask.

Charlie says, "On my poor old Mother's life I won't take a *bar* less than 40 *bars*."

"You must be *divvy*: that *tit* is only worth 20 *bars*."

Christ! Old Charlie spat down on the *puv* and it nearly went over my Luton boots.

"Look here, Butty, give me thirty *bars* or I will get my *yogger* (gun) out and *muller* the *grai*."

"Go on, Charlie, I will toss you for 20 or 30 *bars*."

I toss up a sovereign. Charlie calls 'tails' and the *grai* costs me 30 *bars*. I still know I have a good *grai*. Another thing: when you *chop* (buy) a *grai* you always have the halter, so I *pester* old Charlie, shake *vasts* and go back to my wagon. By that time, Mary-Ann and my son Lazurus have dressed the cobs and put my old horse, Duke, into my wagon. Mary-Ann's trolley is all loaded up and ready for the *drom*.

Let me tell you another thing or two about leaving a *tan* (place), and this is the most dangerous part of travelling. First of all, the *yog* has to be put out. When your *grai* is in the *sharps* (shafts) and about to pull off, everything inside the wagon must be packed away, including all china, etc. This is because pulling off a piece of rough ground will cause things to rattle and break. Also, it can upset the *grai* – a wagon fully loaded can weigh about a tonne, and not just any *grai* is suitable for this work. You must have a *grai* which has been brought up with a wagon. If you were to put an ordinary horse in the wagon, looking back over his blinkers, he will see a very large wagon and think it's too heavy for him to shift. Not knowing that the wagon is hollow, he will often lose heart, but a Romany's *grai* will know that when you give him a command he will lean into his *straps* and slowly take the weight of the wagon and ease it onto the *drom*, not jerking it like other *grais* would and knocking all your *covels* about inside the wagon. Also, a good wagon *grai*, when pulling a wagon up a hill, will not stop until he reaches the top because he knows you will give him a rest then. A horse stopping half way up a hill is a menace and the wagon is in danger of turning over. When a Romany gets a good wagon horse, he's very reluctant to part with it. It knows the family. I myself have seen tiny *chavies* playing under a *grai's* hooves and the *grai* will not stand on them or hurt them. If you have not got a good wagon *grai*, you might as well stay at home.

Before I leave the old common, I do not tell Mary-Ann that I slipped the *chori* (poor) *mush* a pound to help him on his way. That's what we are all in this world for after all, to try and help one another. I tie Charlie's *tit* alongside my *grai*, Duke. This is what we Romanies call a 'sider'. He will learn and help to pull, but he will also learn the Romany ways. We leave Fulmodeston and get onto the Fakenham Road on our way to Grimston. I have *blued* a *grai* in Docking and bought another off old Charlie, and for the time being, I feel *custi*. Life is worth living. I sit on the old wagon board with my *pire* (feet) on the *sharps* – this, in my opinion, is the best seat in the world. You have *loover* in your *putsi*, you have a lovely 15 hand cob pulling you on and at this slow pace you can see the world as you pass it. There's no hurry to get anywhere and you are in this nostalgic mode…let's hope it lasts forever more.

We rest the *grais* about half distance at Rudham. I let the *grais* have a little *chaw* and some *pani*. We send the *chavies* around a *kair* to beg a bit of *pani*. The old *monista* is a right old *groovni* (cow) and refuses us. The *chavies* call at a few more *kenner*s until they find someone a bit more friendly. After a while we are off again on the *drom*. Mid-afternoon we finally arrive onto Grimston common - one of the finest in old Norfolk. Plenty of *needis* use it. You can always stop here a long time; the only trouble is that sometimes, there being large numbers of Romanies, trouble can break out. It happens everywhere.

I draw onto the common and I can see plenty of my 'lations, which is a good sign. My cousin Will Twist is here. His name is Will Lamb but he's known as Will Twist – he stands aside for no one! He is *hatching* here with his old *dai* (mother) Liza Lamb, who's a funny little *rakla*. She is always smoking a clay *swegler* (pipe), but don't be put off by her petite size. Get the wrong side of her and you will regret it for the rest of your life. She is like a wild *matchko* (cat), and she will pull your *yoks* out. Treat her with respect, though, and a finer woman you will be hard pressed to find. Will Twist is also a bit of a handful. Sometimes I have seen Will getting upset with other Romanies because sometimes they can stir him up! Will is known to shout, "Mother, get the suet board out!" This is a wooden board about 12 inches square, used to cut suet and *mass* (meat) up. The old *rakla* will hand it to Will, and he will start to step dance on this small board, much to the amusement of the watching Romanies who have upset him. Faster and faster he dances, diverting the attention of the antagonists. He will then leap through the air like a *beng* (devil) possessed and *coor* the onlookers. Not many folks can handle Will Twist.

A few years ago, I was *rokkering* to a *needi* (traveller) I had met and his dad spoke of Will Twist. He was a legend. Most Romanies are very peaceful and agreeable folk, but you must not upset them! They are very quick to react in anger if they are provoked. When you go to a zoo you do not upset a tiger! Only at your peril. The same with a Romany.

Come on, let's see who else is *hatching* on this old common. To us Lambs, this and Massingham common is our home territory. We have been *hatching* here since I don't know when, far before wagon times. We ourselves have only been in wagons for about fifty years. Before that I have heard my *dadrus* (dad) say we roamed the commons and green lanes with pack horses and bender *tans* (tents) made with hazel rods and a cover over them. Times have changed, but how much longer will we be able to cling to our old wagons? We are a dying race, and the time will come when we can no longer call ourselves Kings of the Commons. Every passing day we are seeing changes, and we are being pushed further to the edge. Soon there will be no place on this earth for us, like I have said before in this book. There is a time and a place: nothing is eternal, and we have had our time!

Christ, what will old Mary-Ann say if she hears me *rokkering* all this *wafti* (bad) talk? Let's go and see Will Twist and his *dai* (mother), Liza Lamb. Cor, that old *chie* can make the best *tograms* (linen pegs) that you would want to see. She is as quick as lightning. This *rarde* (night) I will have a laugh or two with Liza and Will. Who else can I see on this common? Old Lazarus Gray and his *mort* Sophie Gray are here – such good *ratti* (blood). She was a Smith, and you can't get better than that. They are relations of mine, but don't ask me what. I have so many. I can also see Tommy Price – well, I think that's his name – yes, it is him! He will earn himself a nice bit of *loover* here, you see. He is a Romany wagon painter, and I know of nobody better than him with a lark *liner* (a small thin lining brush). He's lining out old Friday Waterfield's *vardo*; what a tradesman. I have seen him using a blade of grass from a *puv* to put a fine line down a spoke on a *bowler* (wheel). That *mush* is a legend. I might, when I get a little more *loover*, ask him to paint my Bill Wright Bowtop wagon. I have it stored in a *Gorgio*'s *gran* (barn), and it's there until I need it.

Another family I can see are a family of Boswells. You can't get much better than these *chals* (boys). I always seem to get on well with a Boswell. Some Romanies are sometimes too cocky for my liking but the Boswells are lovely quiet old boys. My oldest son, Bob, is working the *tit* I *kinned* (bought) off Charlie Wilson. It's coming on nicely and should make a good wagon horse. I will not be surprised if some of these Romany *chals* don't bid me for my *tit*. If I get enough profit, I might *blue* it. This *rardi* we have been invited by old Liza and Will to *scran* (eat) with them. Old Liza makes the best *mass* (meat) pudding you would ever want to eat, so we will be *jelling* (going) over to her *hatch*. Mary-Ann will find old Liza a small gift to show our appreciation. We have also been told to bring our *chavies*, so poor old Liza will want a fair size *mass* pudding. I go over to Tommy Price and Friday Waterfield and ask Tommy what sort of *loover* he would want to paint my wagon.

"How are your getting on, Friday?" I ask.

He says, "I can't get my *loover* to breed like you do, Butty. I hear you have been taking some good *loover* lately for them old *tits* of yours."

"I wish I had," I say, "but they tell me bad times are a-coming. For me they have got here! Have you heard of the idle rich? Well I am one of the idle poor."

"Why, you old minge, Butty; you have got a ton of *loover*."

I ask Tommy to have a look at my Bow-Top when he is out my way. Then I draw back to see what Mary-Ann and the *chavies* are doing. I heat some *pani* in my old *kekubi* (kettle) and have a shave, and then I *tog* myself up. I've got my best silver-topped cane stick. All Romanies like a bit of swagger – you have got to show yourself off. It's our nature. I must say Mary-Ann looks a real *rinkeni* (pretty) lady. The *chavies* are *custi* too. When it is time we all draw over to old Liza's *vardo*. Mary-Ann has taken Liza a small silver photo frame as a gift which she gives her, and the old *rakla* loves it. They tell us to sit down. Will and his *dai* (mother) have laid down some *kas* (hay) and placed some very fine Whitney blankets over the top of it.

Liza says, "Are you ready for your *scran*?"

"I sure am, Liza," I tell her.

With the *mass* pudding we have *puvengros* (potatoes) and some *snoknels* (swedes) served on a Crown Derby platter. Our *churis* (knives) and *fongas* (forks) are the best silver. I think to myself: here I am, old Butty Lamb, sitting on Grimston Common, *scranning* like a *barvalo rye*s (rich gentlemen). The *scran* is washed down with the best *peava* (tea), served again in the finest Crown Derby cup. Old Mary-Ann and Liza light up their *swegglers* (pipes) and I roll a *tibloe* and we sit and enjoy a wonderful *rarde* (night). It has been a feast fit for a King of

England. When at last it is time to leave, all the stars in the Norfolk sky are out. What a good *rarde* we have enjoyed on Grimston common – a Romany's paradise.

We stop on the old Common a few more days, then I get what all Romanies get, the urge to roam. We hate stopping in one place for too long. Mary-Ann, bless her, has made several gross of *tograms* and *faked* (mended) several old *mushes* (umbrellas), so we have a good start when we are ready to get back on the *tober*. My son has also got the young *grai* which I *melled* (bought) off Charlie Wilson, and which is going nicely and is now worth double what I *pestered* Charlie.

After a few days we are ready to roam. When I am ready for the *drom* I am up early. It's the Romany in me; I have got to get up that *tober* and see what's on the side of the *bor* (hedge). At last, we are ready and I have said my farewells to my relations. They have passed messages on to me for their relations if I meet up with them. News travels real fast with us Romanies because we share news and gossip through our grapevine. I am now heading for Thetford Common, so, Reader, if you are out that way, drop in and *dik* (see) me. Also if you have a half *custi grai* I will try and have a *chop* (deal) with you. If you can't find your way to Thetford Common, follow my *patteran* (trail). Good day, pal.

*

Before we leave old Butty Lamb, let me tell you a little more about the Lamb family. Thetford Common was where old Butty Lamb *hatched* during the time of the Great War, 1914-1918. The Army came and took Butty's plain *grais*, and there was nothing you could do about it. They needed horses for the war! You had them, they took them and you were paid a fixed sum. It happened to all other Romanies, and also all others on Thetford Common. I think, at the time, it was the beginning of the decline of the Romany culture as we once knew it. Not only were Romany *grais* taken but Romany *chals* were also taken to fight for the country, which up to then had not treated these folks very well. Butty Lamb was not the only one leaving the *tober*, as lots of old Romanies felt the time was up for them. And so the exodus began. When the war at last ended, Romanies returning back home found it harder to carry on as before, so whole families left the *drom* never to return to it. This left a chasm to be filled by others: and so there were *mumpers* (non-Romanies), basket makers, tinkers, foot pads and a queer mix on the road. A true Romany now had competition – he had to share his Commons and green lanes with the dregs of society. Any minor crime or offence was blamed on the Romanies, so about this time, like an old and weary fox, he went to ground and left the *tober*, leaving it to the mumpers and social drop-outs.

If you have read George Borrow (and I am sure you have), even before 1914, the *drom* was being taken over by a mixture of *turnpike sailors* (tramps). Borrow, if you remember, was stopping at a place called Mumpers Dingle, whose name most certainly suggests that it's a place frequented by *mumpers*. Here also is where he encounters Flaming Jack Bosville, a half-and-half tinker. Ursula, the Romany *chie* who befriends Borrow, says her folk hate people who live in caravans and basket makers. So you see, even then, there was much competition for a place on the *drom*. When the Romanies were out on the *drom*, their *ratti* was pure but as soon as they moved into *bricks* they started to mix with *Gorgios* and this is what started the demise of the whole Romany culture as we once knew it. I think the last true domain of the true Romany was in Wales. Families there were more isolated in this rugged and remote country and they did not come into so much contact with *Gorgios*. They, I think, were the last to succumb to the diluting of the true black *ratti* of the Romanies. Even today a true Welsh Romany still *rokkers* good Romany. It's only a short time before even this last domain will be broken and lost forever.

The Romanies were being pushed further off the *drom* and finally realised there was nowhere to go and then, I think, that is when a lot of true Romanies decided to call it a day. It seems like the *Gorgios* had won. If they did it was a very hollow victory, for even today they are still here – not in their full glory – but they remain and I think they will always remain. So we have old Butty Lamb and his family leaving the *drom* in 1914. He moved his family to North Walsham, where he and old Mary-Ann would see out the rest of their days at the *hatching tan* (stopping place). He stopped at Bradfield Road in North Walsham. It was owned by a fellow by the name of Jordan, a relation of Ben Jordan. One of these Jordans *rommed* a Waterfield, a good Romany family. This same *puv* (field) was the home for years of old Miney Slender who had a scrap yard on it and she also built her bungalow on it. It's still lived in by her granddaughter Lily Slender, a lovely *rakla*. After a while, Butty bought his own *puv* at Catch Pit Lane, North Walsham. He pulled his Leonards of Soham Reading *vardo* on and here he remained for the rest of his life. I think old Butty passed away in about 1945. His *mort* Mary-Ann passed away about 1958. My uncle, Winks Lamb, continued to live there along with his brother, Bert Lamb. Even today, part of the *puv* is home to Bert Lamb's family, who still live there in *trailers*.

Just before I move on to other stories, let me tell you about the 1914 war. If you remember, the Army would take all the best *grais* from the Romanies. This could not continue as they would not have any *custi grais*, so this is what Romanies did at this time. They *blued* all their plain coloured horses and started to breed black and white piebalds. The Army could not use these as the colour was not right. Look at any Army cavalry photo: do you see any piebald horses? The answer is no. So, you see, a Romany is still very cunning in his thinking. He has learned how to survive.

What happened to the rest of the Lamb family? Starting with

the oldest, Bob Lamb moved away down to Essex and Lambs remain in Essex to this day. Lazarus, another son, sadly passed away quite young with TB. If you remember, he left his brother, Winks, his horse and trolley. Winks, however, was not much of a horseman, and there's a little tale here. Winks used his brother's horse and trolley to collect a little bit or two of *rust* round the town here, but Winks let the poor old *grai* get down and it was poor. It was in a bad state. One day, Winks was coming up Grammar School Lane in the town with a load of *rust* on the old trolley. Living in a bungalow on the lane is an old RSPCA woman. Past her *kair* goes Winks with the poor old *tit*. The old *rakla* spots Winks and reports him to the RSPCA. Winks sees the old *rakla* watching him so he nips down to our place on Spa Common and puts one of our fine *grais* into his trolley. Winks was only home a little while before the old *rakla* and two officers turned up, asking Winks to show them his horse. Winks opens the old stable door for them to inspect the *grai*. The two officers were amazed to see such a fine horse. The two officers turned on the old *rakla* and wanted to know why she was wasting their time. The old *rakla* did not know what to say and Winks had a good result. Winks had to have the old *grai* put down and after that Winks kept away from *grais*.

Mother had a brother called Archie, but most of his family called him Chinner. He lived over Kings Lynn way, not far from Grimston Common where his father Butty Lamb liked to *hatch*. Chinner for years lodged with a nice old *rakla*. He mostly got his living making *tograms*, and he made thousands of them. He had a brother, Daniel Lamb, whose nickname was Butcher. He was a bricklayer and worked and lived here in North Walsham. Albert Lamb was another; his nickname was Petty. He dealt mostly in *gunners* (sacks) and became quite wealthy dealing in them. He and his *mort* would call down at ours regularly on a Sunday afternoon with his son Maurice, who now lives in Lincolnshire. Albert's other son was Johnny, but sadly he passed away about two years ago. He lived to a good age – I think he was 92. Albert also had three daughters, one of whom *rommed* a showman, Charlie Stocks. Another sister's *rom* had a garage at Swaffham. Lastly, the sister called Molly Lamb would come to North Walsham by train, borrow a *treader* (bike) from my mother and would *hawk* her *covels* around the North Walsham area. All the Lambs were very good salespeople.

Now we come down to Bert Lamb. I have already mentioned him in this book. He dealt most of his life in scrap until later in life when Bert, like many other old Romany *chals*, got into the antique trade. His sons and their daughters still live in modern *trailers* on the same *puv* that old Butty Lamb bought many years ago. The sons, like their *dadrus*, still buy and sell scrap and antiques, thus keeping up the family tradition. The last Lamb brother we now come to is Robert Lamb, always known as Hobby. He was a funny old *coover* (thing). Hobby was a bit of a Don Juan as he liked the *monistas* (women). Hobby once told me how he helped the war effort; he said all the young fellows had gone off to war and they left behind very lonely and frustrated wives who needed a little love and attention. So Hobby was there, helping the war effort! Hobby, like his brother Albert, dealt mostly in *gunners*. Over at Mundesley lived an old *givengro* who promised Hobby all his *rust* when he retired. The time eventually came and Hobby called me to help him. I was over at Mundesley carting away scrap on my old *moulder*. I was at it for the best part of a week. All the time I was carting, Hobby was filling his van with metal which he was picking out of the scrap. When we had finished, Hobby said to the old *mush*, "Let's go inside your house and I will square you up." Off they went, and a little later Hobby appeared with the old mush and then Hobby told me, "I paid him out. I gave him £8." Christ, Hobby had *monged* (begged) it. The *rust* and the metal came to over £300 and that was years ago. The whole Lamb family were good operators. The old *mush* was pleased with the little bit of *loover* which Hobby gave him.

Back to the Lamb family – Butty Lamb had four daughters. Milly Lamb *rommed* Tater Billy. His real name was Billy Hudson, and they lived over Holt way. Milly would do a little *tatting* (collecting rags). Tater Billy would sharpen lawn mowers and shears, etc. He was a funny sort of *mush*. Daisy Lamb was another sister, and she *rommed* George Adams, a *flat mush* (non-Romany). They lived out at Dereham. The oldest sister was Ada Lamb and she was married to Charlie Gray. She left Charlie Gray and finished up living not far from us at Sloley near Worstead. Her sons Gilly, Harry, Charlie, Russell, Felix and Stanley were very well known in Romany circles. My mother, Mary Lamb, *rommed* Edgie Harmer, a horse dealer, and we all lived in an old railway carriage down here on Spa Common. I still live there, though sadly the old carriage is gone. I live in a *kenner* I had built in 1991. Another sad fact: almost all the Lambs around here are buried in North Walsham and it's tradition to use Murrell Cork of North Walsham. So when my time is up and the Grim Reaper comes looking for me, it will be Murrell Cork of North Walsham for me! Christ, you don't want just anyone carrying you into St Nicholas Church; it's nice to know who's handling you. I must stop this! Talking about *mullering* makes my old hair on the back of my head stand up on end! Let's find something better, what do you say? This book is supposed to be about my Romany life, so let's *rokker* about it.

Come Buy My Wares!

I have told you about when I was doing a bit of *rust* dealing as well as buying up old rags and antiques, but what else is there? You name it and I think I may have done it. After the old scrap game, I got into spraying old farm buildings in black bitumen. What a dirty old job; you could earn good *loover* but the aggravation you got was a nightmare. The bitumen you were spraying was thinned down with diesel and it did not last on a building too long so you did not get many repeat orders. Also a few old *Gorgios* were getting a little p****d off with me, so I gave this lark up. One good little number I had going was exporting to the USA large quantities of antique woodworking tools. You could earn top dollar doing this. Sometimes, some of my American buyers would come over here to see me. I remember quite well one Sunday morning I met a lovely couple, a man and his wife all the way from New York! They stayed in the Castle Hotel in Norwich and I drove up there to meet them on a Sunday morning. I sold them a complete van full of antique tools. This deal came to a few thousand pounds. After that, I had my photo taken with them with Norwich's Norman castle in the background.

Like everything, nothing lasts forever, and several other *mushes* started to get into this game. Stuff got harder to source, so I got out while the going was still good. I then started to buy other antique collectables for the USA market. I would sell direct to American dealers and I never had a middle man, because if you do he will want to earn more *loover* than you. I have sold cast iron implement seats over in the States – I was selling plenty of these for £100 a pop in the 1970s. Good *loover* then. Old animal traps: now this was a good earner. I would find American trap collectors old traps: fox, badger, bird, rat, mantraps, etc. When these started to get in short supply the Americans asked me to find new modern traps, so I would call in around here at ironmongers' shops and buy up their entire stocks of new traps and export them to the States, selling them for top dollar.

I once bought an altar cloth which was in lovely gold embroidery needlework. It came, so I was told, from Somerton Church near Martham. I sold it to a lady collector of textiles in Texas. The lady who I bought it off said with a laugh that it might have been used at the funeral of Robert Hales, 'The Norfolk Giant', in Somerton Church. In the Seventies I got into another nice little earner. I was drinking one night ("What do you mean you were drinking one night? You were always drinking!") ...anyway, I was in the Rising Sun, a small ale house in North Walsham. Old Lou Lancaster was the landlord, and he was a *custi* old *guero* (man). When this *kitchema* closed, Doreen and Ray Wright bought it and opened it up as a bric-a-brac shop, bless them. F**k, I keep wandering off the path: Mike, boy, concentrate! It was on a Saturday night, when in walked a nice well-to-do *mush* who looked like he was not short of a few *John Bradburys* in his *putsi* (pocket). If you are like me, you have to grasp chances whenever they come, and don't let them go. I bought the *rye* a *scimish* and started to operate on him. It seems he had just bought himself a holiday *kair* only just down the road from my place. I started to *rokker* to him and find out his full SP (starting prices). It seems he was living up in the *smoke* (London) and he came from a very *barvalo* (rich) family. This was getting interesting, Mike! You could say I was moving in for the kill. I found out he also had an antique shop in London. He was married with a nice *mort* and two small *chavies*. To cut a long story short, or to kill two *chiriclos* (birds) with one stone, this *mush* was meant for me. He was looking for a contact down here to source him *covels*. This would suit me real fine. I had just found myself a *custi rye* with plenty of *loover* in his *bin*, and that night we came together!

At that time, things were happening in London. This *mush* was part of the Chelsea set – Carnaby Street, Mary Quant – between us we could do great business, which we certainly did.

He told me what he was looking for and I would get on the case and Bob's your Aunt (I think I got that wrong...never mind), there was gold in these hills. I did well over a few years with this guy. By the way, his name, like mine, was Mike! I don't think I have ever met a bad Mike and I don't think I've ever met a good one! Every month he would come to Norfolk down the old A11 and bring me my *John Bradburys*. I would buy him antiques, paintings, ceramics...you name it, I was there like a flea on a hedgehog. If I could not always buy him stuff I would introduce him to other dealers and have a cut off them. One time when he was staying down here, he spotted an old horse-drawn farm wagon which he liked very much, so I started to buy him some. I bought him so many, I soon filled his large garden with them. He then went and bought a two acre field next to my *kair*, and then I went to town! I started to fill the field up with wagons. Back in that day, you could buy a good one for £10 and Mike would *pester* me about fifty *bars* a pop. But remember what I try to keep telling you – every dog has its day! Nothing lasts forever. Mike saw a manor house several miles away from here and he bought it. Myself and two more men used our lorries to transport all Mike's wagons, etc. He also had a nice early old kite wagon I had sold him. We, for a time, continued to deal together but, sadly, on his way up to Norfolk one day he was involved in a rather serious car accident, and he sold up and never returned. So the moral of the story is, never put all your *yoros* (eggs) in one basket. I had to look out then for another Sugar Daddy. Plenty of those old farm wagons which I sold to Mike would fetch up to nearly a thousand pounds and there was little old me monging (begging) them for £10 a pop.

*

Loover today has no value. When I first got started in reclamations in the Seventies, it happened by chance, like a lot of things. It was all about being in the right place at the right time. Around then I was buying up old oak timber and selling on to a firm in Norfolk to make reproduction furniture. I had just bought a large amount of oak beams from a *rye* at an old stately hall not far away from me. On buying a second lot of timber, the *rye* said to me,

"Before you take that old oak out of my buildings, get out the Norfolk red bricks."

I said, "What can I do with them, Master?"

"They are valuable; you can sell them," he replied.

"Can I?" I said.

He said, "I want £8 per thousand for them."

"If that's what you want, Master, leave it to me and I will see what I can do with them".

I thought – who the f**k would want them? But I knew a *mush* who was a builder and had a word in his *kaun* (ear), so I asked him,

"Bob, does anyone buy old Norfolk red bricks?"

"'Course they do; you can get £80 per thousand for them."

This got my old brain box a-ticking, and I thanked Bob for his help. Back I went to the *barvalo rye* (rich gent) and he took me around and showed me some old brick buildings. He told me to help myself, so I made a start into the reclamation trade. I recruited my brother-in-law, David Sutton, from Briston. I am afraid that sadly he passed away a few years ago. Also in my demolition team was my *mort*; her name was Hazel Jane, and she could work like a *mush* and swear like one, too! So we started to get the bricks from these old Norfolk buildings. When we started, we did not know how to clean the bricks, nor did we know how to stack them or how even to count them. To put it mildly, we knew f**k all! Slowly we learned, and it turned into a good earner. At this estate, as we finished a building, the *rye* would find us more to take down. In the end I was maybe the biggest supplier of Norfolk red bricks in the eastern counties. I have bought barns and houses all over Norfolk and sometimes down in Suffolk. I have bought them from lords and other titled people. I have also sold bricks to royalty, but I myself like to deal with common working people. You know that they will not try to tuck you up, but the higher you climb the ladder the more devious they get.

I once bought part of a large period house from a guy whose father was a baron. I knew he was a brick short of a load. For all his pedigree, he did not have a pot to p**s in. I paid him and when we went to start the job he had wrecked a large deal of it, so I had a go at him. He said, "I did not do it Mike!"

"Who the f**k did?" I replied.

He said, "It was Mexicans."

"Mexicans?" I said.

"Yes, they broke into my home last night and I had to chase them away with a sword."

This bloody house is in sleepy rural Cromer-on-Sea! What the f**k are Mexicans doing here in Cromer? I soon found out that the baronet was on drugs and also he liked a bit of *sherbert* (drink). Don't I meet them? Ha! Mexicans in Cromer. I held my *chib* (tongue) and carried on with the demolition. I finished up earning over a few years good *loover* off this *dinilo*. You have to take them as they come; you can't pick and choose who you deal with.

Now let's get on to another subject. Let's talk about shithouses. I don't mean eccentric people: I mean shithouses. Right, let me put you in the frame or, in plain terms, I will mark your card for you. In Norfolk a few years ago, nearly every village had a school. I bet you did not know this; did you? I think it was in the Nineties that the Education Authority decided that all schools

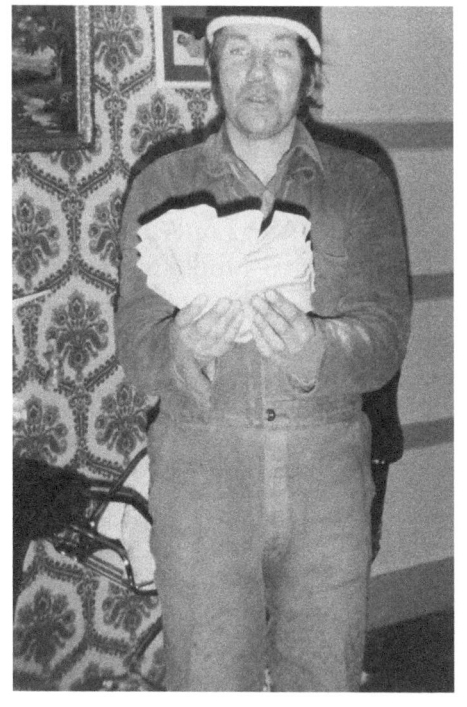

A younger Mike Harmer brandishes a fistful of Bradburys after a very successful deal.

should have inside toilets, and why not?! So all the outside toilets (let's not use the other nasty word) were made redundant. Now, this is where old matey here, Mike Harmer, comes in. I got in with a top school inspector for Norfolk; what a lovely old *mush* was he! He got me to demolish all these old Victorian red brick toilets, most of which were made with first class Norfolk Reds. Each school had a boys' and girls' toilets, and most of them had a brick shed attached to them with good slates or tiles on the roofs. These were good earners – you could *mong* them, and sometimes they would pay me to take them down. I must have demolished hundreds of them. So, Reader, shithouses are not always bad!

One of the best jobs I did was in the Eighties at Fakenham at a large red brick Victorian maltings. It stood on an acre of ground. A pal of mine, George Banks, and I did it together. George now lives at Fakenham. We were six to eight months taking down this malting. There were thousands of bricks in it. The ground floor of this maltings had 11,000 9 by 9 pamments on it. Next to the maltings was another big site with lots of brick buildings on it which I demolished a little later. The bricks in these buildings were from Lord Hastings's Barney brickyard. These are some of the best bricks in Norfolk. My house here at North Walsham is built from them. I built my *kair* in 1990. Also I once had a brick order from a *mush* who had a contract to supply Norfolk red bricks for a dockside development in London. He phoned me and said, "Can you supply me with good Norfolk reds?"

I said, "I will try – how many do you want?"

He replied, "I want a million."

"How many?" I replied.

"A million," he repeated.

F**k, I have not got that many in my yard. I said to him I would have to demolish most of North Walsham to get that many. He told me about this contract he had. He wanted a million over a period of time. I said to him, "If I were to supply you I would not have another customer." So I turned him down. You do not want all your *yoros* in one *kipsi* (basket). I have seen plenty of old boys start up in the reclamation trade and then fade away. The only other reclaim trader who has been doing it for as long as me is James Webster at Tower Materials down at Mendlesham in Suffolk. He and his wife Ann are a lovely couple – salt of the earth.

Crafty Folk & Cannon Balls

Let's move on from demolition, though I am 78 years old and I still do it. Pack it in Mike; hang up your hammer and bolster! Before the next part of the book, let me list for you some of the things I have done. Here goes....you will find it a long list. Can any of you out there beat this? Paperboy, farm worker, watercress seller, holly seller, scrap dealer, waste paper dealer, poly sack dealer, paper bag merchant, *togram* maker, *tatter*, wood seller, fence maker, tar sprayer, antique dealer, trap dealer, woodworking tool dealer, car dealer, demolition contractor, reclamation dealer, wagon maker, author.

Let's leave all this b***s**t and *rokker* about old and odd characters...interesting people. Of course you did not know that my father Edgie was a bit of an athlete. Yes, that's right, Edgie could move himself about a bit. In my last book, Ikey Wright was mentioned. He, if you remember, was a dealer come small farmer from North Walsham. Anyway, let's push on – if not, this old book will soon be as big as Tolstoy's War and Peace. You won't be able to get it through your letterbox. Edgie and Ikey had a love/hate relationship over the years. I think hate was the biggest percentage. Up our road was the pub called The Anchor. Anyhow, one day a lady living up our road heard a hell of a commotion going on in her yard. It was Edgie and Ikey Wright, who had had a falling out over something and they were about to have a *chingaripen* (fight) in her yard, although I don't know why. They decided to settle the *lav chingaripen* (argument) with a race. Edgie, like I said, was quite small and nimble, whereas Ikey was a little on the plump side and did not look much like a runner. The rules were drawn up that they would start from The Anchor and run down the *drom* to our place, The Windy City. They would touch the gate and race back to The Anchor to prove who was the best man. They had a good audience standing and watching, all from The Anchor.

Someone started the race off, and Edgie was out of his blocks like Linford Christie. He was getting over the ground fast while Ikey was trailing behind. The distance from The Anchor would be, I think, about 400 yards, making the course about 800 yards, or just under a half mile. Edgie touched the old Windy City gate and doubled back on the home straight to The Anchor. Almost there, Edgie began to falter. He had gone too soon. Sensing this, Ikey piled on the pace and just before the finish Ikey flew past Edgie like a bat out of hell. After that, Edgie could not believe Ikey Wright had beaten him. Edgie had to settle for a silver medal, and Ikey got gold and was champion of Spa Common.

*

Who else have we got around these parts? Let's not forget Don Farrow; they don't come more eccentric than him. Don is still about in North Walsham. You may not know this, but Don has some Romany *ratti*. Don's old *purodia* (grandmother) was, I think, a daughter of old Triana Gay, whose *rom* was a Romany by the name of Boman Gay. She has a sister called Genti and her brother was Sammy Gay: remember him in my last book? He was the one who kept *shooshis* (rabbits) in the cellars in the old butchery in North Walsham. So, you see, even Don Farrow has a little Romany *ratti*. Don's grandfather was Carl Farrow, and he had a blacksmith's forge in Hall Lane and was a part time fireman. Don has a vast knowledge of local history; if ever you want to know about past events, ask Don Farrow.

Let me tell you about Don. Years ago, he owned a little Singer car. He had never had a full driving licence so Bob Amis, a local scallywag (to put it mildly) started to teach Don to drive, Don slapped on the old 'L' plates and Bob sat beside Don with Ruby Farrow (Don's mother) in the back and off they went for a little driving tuition. Don drove the little Singer to White Horse Common.

About a mile in, Bob shouted, "Pull in here, Don." It was the White Horse pub: "I need a drink...give me some money, Don."

Bob left Don and his mum in the Singer. After a while Bob emerged from the pub, saying, "Right, Don, get driving." After about a mile they arrived at Spa Common.

"Stop," said Bob, "I am still thirsty."

They pulled up outside The Anchor, and in went Bob. Same thing – after a time out came Bob, and off they went again to The Bluebell pub, about a half mile away. It did not take Don too long to catch on to Bob Amis. The only tuition that Don got was a grand tour of all the local pubs.

Another tale I can tell you is about Bob Amis, my sister Maureen and I. This was before we left school, many years ago. We went broadbean picking for old John Howes, a farmer from Briggate near Worstead. The bean field was right beside the railway station. We had not been there long when a steam train pulled up at the station and off the train jumped Bob Amis, Don Farrow's mother, Ruby, and her son, Russell. Bob Amis had just got himself a little slave labour. I thought William Wilberforce had abolished slavery in 1865, but perhaps he did not tell Bob Amis! Bob marched his bean pickers into the field and instructed them to work. When picking the beans, you picked them from the stalks into a pail then you tipped them into large sacks. This was very hard work. If Ruby or Russell showed signs of slacking, Bob would shout at them and try to make them work harder. At the end of a very long day, Ruby and Russell asked Bob how much money they had earned. He replied,

"You have not earned anything."

"Why not?" they asked.

"Because," said Bob, "I have given you a nice day out. You had a ride on the train; it was like a holiday for you."

Bob collected their money from John Howes, and they never got a *nook* (penny). Christ, you had to watch them old fly Norfolk boys; they would have the laces out of your *chokkers* (shoes). Bless them!

*

I knew Russell Farrow, Don's brother, when we were at school together – he was a lovely old boy. He worked at a hospital down in Cromer. He had various days off when would work for me. Several years ago I was demolishing a house in Cromer and my only means of getting the brick rubble away was by a small Ford Dexta tractor and trailer which I borrowed from Major Gurney at Northrepps Hall. He wanted the rubble so I borrowed his little tractor and trailer. The rubble had to be loaded by hand. One morning I left Russell to fill the trailer while my brother-in-law, David Sutton, and I delivered some tiles. Russell was a strong old boy and he soon got stuck into the task. We were gone a little longer than expected and when we got back Russell was still packing the rubble onto the trailer. I have never seen a trailer loaded with so much! You see, no one had told Russell to stop, so he kept loading it on.

I was a *dinolo* to drive the tractor up to Major Gurney's farm. Coming out of Cromer is a long, steep hill, and up we went, me and my little blue tractor. She was really starting to struggle with that load. I kept changing down the gears; I was only half way up the hill and I was in first gear! The front of the tractor kept lifting up off the ground and I came to a standstill. I had about twenty cars behind, blowing their bloody horns. I was in the shit! I had to reverse back down the old hill, right down to Cromer. I must have had 6 tonnes on a 3 tonnes trailer. Lucky the *gavvers* (police) were not about. How I got back to the demolition site I will never know.

Another time, Russell and I were taking down an old brick building just the other side of Reedham Ferry. We had just loaded my old *moulder* up with pantiles. I jumped in and drove out onto the *tober*. The opposite side was an ex-public house with a low pantiled roof beside it. My old *moulder* had a hiab crane on it and I forgot to put it in, so it was sticking well out from the moulder. Out I went and turned near the pub. Just missing that (but not the low building), I stripped rows of the tiles off it, only just missing the gable end of the building. In a bit of luck, the people of the ex-pub were out, so Russell and I had to do a little re-roofing. It took nearly all the tiles I had on my old *moulder*. I did not earn much *loover* that day! I had almost demolished part of the old pub.

*

Here is another tale I must tell you...that is, if you want to hear it. You can't wait, can you? A few years ago, I was demolishing the lovely old Angel Hotel in North Walsham. It brings tears to my *yoks* to think I was the bastard who knocked down my favourite old *kitchema* in North Walsham. I have sunk several *shants* in there. The only thing I have to remember the old Angel Hotel by is on my living room floor. I have the old boards which came from the Angel. Sometimes on a dark and cold old winter's night with the cruel north east winds howling from the North Sea and freezing rain rattling the old window panes, down below in my living room I think I can hear the clinking of glasses and hear ghostly laughter. Maybe I am going light in the head or maybe it is hallucinations. Anyway, let's forget all this ghostly crap and return to the tale which I must tell you!

When we were demolishing the old Angel, in one of the old outhouses I found a rather large and heavy cannon ball – it was a *soler*! I put it behind the seat of my old transit truck and thought some old simple *Gorgio* might buy it. Everybody should have a cannon ball: have you got one, Reader? Back to the yarn. A nice *mush* I knew came onto the Angel Hotel site and I *fenced* him some building materials and I let him have my old truck to take his stuff home. I don't know where it happened, but he was on his way home to Alby, about eight miles from North Walsham, when he came to a junction and put his foot on the old truck's brakes. From out of the blue this bloody great cannon ball came flying out! It hit the *mush* behind the ankle. He nearly crashed the old truck and he thought it had broken his leg! Christ, was he savage when he brought my old truck back. I said,

"What's up chap?"

"What's up? I will tell you what's up. When you borrow a truck, you don't expect a cannon ball to fly out and hit you!"

After a while he could see the funny side, and when I see him we still laugh about it. I wonder if it was one of Lord Nelson's from the old victory. You just don't know, do you?

While we are on the subject of cannon balls, on the opposite side of the old Angel Hotel was The Rising Sun. The landlord was Lou Lancaster. Inside the old pub near the door Lou had a large old cannon ball that had been cut in half and which Lou used for a door stop. Lou had a competition going. If you could pick up the cannon ball with one hand, Lou would give you a *shant*. He told me that in all the time he had had the pub, only one *mush* lifted it. Lou said he had hands on him as big as dinner plates. Years ago, most old pubs had little tests for their customers. Over at Stalham Harnser one night, for example, they had a competition to see who could eat the most longshores, the local herrings. The old landlord had a good supply of longshores. The old boys would grill them on a grid iron over the hot coals on the open fire, which must have stunk the pub out. This particular night the competition was won by a little *mush* by the name of Sam

Bean from Sutton. He somehow managed to eat 16 longshores; that's a good feast for anyone. Sam Bean was a nice old boy, and in later years he would work at Stalham sale. When he was younger, he was a drover - it is not the most well-known of trades these days but back then it was a person who drove animals across the country on foot. Look here, Reader, I think I am getting off the main theme of this damn book! It's supposed to be about my Romany life, not talking about bloody cannon balls and longshore herring. I know you want to hear about the old Romany *chals* and *chies*.

Romany Ways And Vardoes

Since writing my last book, I have been totally amazed at the number of people I have met who think they have got a little Romany *ratti* in their veins. I sold a book to a very eminent and important Queen's counsellor and he thought (or hoped) he had Romany *ratti*. What's up with these people? All of a sudden everyone wants to be a Romany. My theory is that people of today are living in a very stressful environment. Mostly it's the 9 to 6 brigade. They are under severe emotional stress and need some sort of escape, and I think the romanticism of Romany life is the appealing factor in their search for their utopia of stress-free indulgence. If these folks could go back quite a few years they would find a race of these wonderful people, the Romanies, having to endure everything that mankind could throw at them. The Romany people would be harassed, abused and sometimes even be transported and finally executed. I wonder if the 9 to 6 brigade would like that? Would this help their endeavour to be a romantic care-free Romany out on the *drom*, sharing a stress-free existence? I think not!

Today, the Romany is held in high esteem by these romantic theologians. However, the *tober* has not always been that golden highway which leads off into a golden sunset. It was sometimes very cruel and very soul destroying, but we have survived, despite George Borrow's doubts that we would. We are still here. We are survivors, so let's rejoice in our own endeavour to reach that golden heaven.

In years long gone, in biblical times, a curse was imposed on the Romany race. It started with the crucifixion of Jesus Christ. The Romans got a Romany tinker to forge the four nails, which were to secure the Saviour to the Cross. The Romany tinker set about his task and was just about to finish the fourth nail when, to his utter dismay, he realised it was intended for Christ. So the poor

Romany tinker fled, taking with him the fourth nail. After that, a curse was put upon the Romany race and they were pursued and banished from every continent of the world. From that time forth, we have always been branded as thieves and vagabonds. Even today, they are still searching for the fourth nail. Look at any depiction of the crucifixion and you will see only three nails. You see, Reader, the Romanies are still getting the blame over two thousand years later. Will we ever win?

*

Crikey, how much bigger is this old *lil* (book) going to get? It reminds me, at school when you had misbehaved, they would make you stay in class and write out 500 times some meaningless *lavs* (words). Anyway, come on: let's get back to our old Romany *pralas* (brothers).

You must agree that the Romany life which we all knew is now almost completely gone. True Romanies of today still try to keep up old traditions and beliefs, and you will still find them at various *wellgorus* (fairs). Some still cling to their *grais* but that life is mostly gone. When a Romany moves out and leaves his old *vardo*, he is not a proper Romany in the truest sense anymore. We all like to hold on to things which are indeed part of our culture and heritage, but I think the true Romany will always try to cling to his inner beliefs and upbringings. Let me write down in this book my feelings of changes which have occurred over the later years.

Let's go back in time to when we left our homeland, the sub-continent of India, over a thousand years ago. The wandering tribes of nomadic Asian Romanies slowly spread across the face of the globe. I think, as we were told by academic scholars of the time, people were fascinated by this strange race of people. As time wore on, fascination started to turn into fear and then into hate. Let's face the facts – it seems as they slowly made their way across the world, to all purposes they were a somewhat frightful race. They also started to court public opinion against themselves by stealing and begging, and in all they seemed a despicable race. By stirring up public opinion against themselves so, they are, I think, faced with a dilemma. The host nations are growing wary of this wild and sometimes frightening rabble. And so they have tried to rid themselves of these people, and not always in a gentle manner. It must have taken several years before these large groups of nomadic travellers started to realise that to remain in these countries (which they had virtually invaded), they must adjust and start to gain the trust of their fellow man. Over the years they have achieved this, becoming more genteel and placid in their approach to hosts. They have started to blend in...to be humble...to become as we know them today – romantic Romanies travelling the old byways and wide open spaces. They are not being menaces – not stirring up hate and resentment, but portraying himself to others that Romanies are assets to their country of choice.

If you forgive us Romanies for any misdemeanours which in the past have been committed against you, I think that at last people can see the truly romantic side of the Romany. You have taken from us our commons and green lanes but you cannot take our hearts away. Let's remain here in idyllic peace for another thousand years. I have stated my views; whether you agree or disagree, I humbly respect your worthy opinion. Most things about the Romanies have in the past been written by some very clever academic scholars, so what can a simple old Romany *chal* like myself add? I can only offer you small pieces of Romany lore which maybe our learned scholars have missed or simply dismissed by thinking they are of no importance.

As I mentioned in my last book, the Romany male is like the large and aggressive male lion in a pride of lions. He is loud! He is regal! He tries to dominate but he fails: the lioness of the pride is the one who dominates. She and her sisters go on the hunt and bring back the bounty while the male waits for his Sunday lunch. Just like a Romany *mush* the Romany *chies* are the breadwinners. They go out each day with their *kipsies* (baskets) loaded up with *covels*, most of which they have made themselves. They also rule the *hatching tan* and do most of the *buty* (work) while the Romany *guero* (man) sits, maybe looking after the young *chavies*, keeping a *yok* on the wagon and *grais*. The Romany *raklas* would also look after the *loover*. In most cases, the Romany *mush* always had *loover* in his *putsi*. Romanies, as many of you know, had strong ritual customs, most of which are still observed today. Romanies are *thrashed* (frightened) of the *mullo* (dead) and will not handle a dead body, and that's why years ago most of the possessions of the *mullered* were *yogged* (burned) as well as the deceased's wagon. It was also customary to get rid of the deceased's *grais* and break up all their china and glassware and personal things. The only things that were kept would be *sunakai* (gold) or *rap fawnees* (silver rings).

I was told by my mother that she was told that some Romanies had wayside burials for their folk. It would be on an old common or green lane and often they would plant a thorn tree on the *mulleno hev* (grave). I have read in books of Romanies burying their *mullo* on Mousehold Heath in Norwich, as this was a very important Romany *hatching tan* of years gone by. Most, if not all, Romanies are very religious and will *rom* and have baptisms in a *congri* (church). I don't think (and this, I must say, is my opinion) that any other race on God's earth maintains the love and bond with their children as the English Romany does. Only the Italians come anywhere close to them. Major crime in Romany culture is virtually non-existent. Rape and murder are not part of their nature. Reader, don't think I am painting the English Romany in glossy white colour; in all races you have your criminal elements. In fact, maybe of late there has been a rise in minor incidents – I think this may be due to mixed *ratti* which has infused our Romany race.

Lets now *rokker* about the language of the *rom* (Romany). It's very diluted and fragmented; it remains only as jargon. It is so anglicised that it is hard to form even one sentence together. I am pleased to say, however, that if you happen to be in their company (and I hope you are at some time), you will hear Romany *chals* still using *lavs* (words). Maybe it will be at a horse fair or maybe just in a *kitchema*, but you will hear it. In writing this book and my first book, I have used a fair number of Romany words. I know it breaks up the sentences, but I say let's use them...let's not let them *muller*. Try to imagine the old Romanies using the same *lavs* (words) but in complete sentences; it was truly wonderful.

*

Now, once again lets get back on to one of my favourite subjects: *vardoes*...how I love them! If you are a Romany there is nothing more breathtaking than to see a *custi* wagon in all its regal splendour. Unfortunately, the most you will ever see will be housed in a country folk museum. It's still a lovely sight, but not as nice as seeing one *hatched* on an old wayside common, being used and breathing life. This is the true way to see an English Romany wagon, not in a museum. It's the same as looking at sad animals in a zoo. My friend, go to a horse fair if you are very lucky and see one still *hatched* in a green lane. Stop and savour the moment; a better sight you will never see.

Believe me, we all associate Romanies with *vardoes*, but this is certainly not always the case. The Romanies were the last to live in wagons and they were the last to leave. Vardoes came about, it is believed, around the latter part of the 19th Century. At first they were large cumbersome things, certainly not like horse wagons. It is thought that travelling showmen were some of the first to use them, but the English Romany would closely follow the showmen. At fairs, Romanies would sell their *grais*, and a few of them would have small booths or stalls. I think the Romany saw something he liked and when he started to earn just that little more *loover*, he had the means to go up to a wagon builder and have one made to his own design. It was much smaller so it could be pulled by one horse, and I think this is how the English Romany wagon evolved.

Another thing – both the showman and the Romany sometimes travelled the same *tober*. There is, I think, no connection. They are very allied but a completely different race of people. All Romany wagons have the same layout inside because a wagon demands an economic use of space within. The iron stove which a Romany calls a 'boo' is always on the left side as you enter. The reason for this is that the stove pipe that protrudes through the roof is on the offside, away from the hedge and trees. The bed is at the back of the wagon. A more comfortable and cosy home would be hard to find.

Let me talk you through the various types of wagons. Reader, here is a little tip for you: if you happen to have the chance to look inside a wagon, always look at the door and see which way it opens. This will tell you who had the wagon made when it was new. If the door opens outwards, it was made for a Romany. If it opens inwards, it was made for a showman. No one knows why but it is a fact. All wagons made before about 1910 would be much taller than later ones. After circa 1910 wagons had a 'Mollycroft' or glass raised window light installed to give added light and to give more headroom.

Let's now take a look at some of these *vardoes*. We will start with the 'Reading'. No one knows with certainty how it got its name, but it's mostly thought that Dunton of Reading, who was a most important wagon builder of their time, could have inspired it. I think that the 'Reading' is the most favoured *vardo* by Romanies. Next, we come to the 'Ledge', sometimes called a cottage wagon. Its dimensions are about the same as the 'Reading'. The wagon body is about 10 feet 6 inches and just over 6 feet wide. The weight of these two wagons when loaded would be somewhere in the region of a tonne. On Norfolk's flat *tobers*, one good 15 hand cob would manage it with ease. On more hilly terrain, a sider would help with pulling the wagon. The 'Ledge' wagon, as its name suggests, has protruding ledges on either side of the body. Built on this outside ledge are two fancy spindle wood cupboards mostly used by Romanies to house their bantams and game cocks. The room layout is virtually the same as the Reading. Both these two wagons have a high floor bed – that's to say that the wagon has high wheels and they run on the outside of the wagon. That is why these types of wagons were favoured by Romanies, as the wagons could traverse over rough ground and cross fords.

The next wagon we will deal with is called a 'Burton'. Here again, we have the name of a place: Burton-on-Trent. Around these parts were some good wagon builders. The Burton again has the same room layout, but this wagon has much smaller wheels. These run under the wagon's body making it prone to turning over when on angled ground. Wagons with large wheels on the outside are much more stable and the 'Burton' wagon, when it was made, was most certainly made for showmen and fairground folk. These people stopped on flat pitches. The possibility of overturning would not affect them. In almost all 'Burtons' the doors will open inwards, unlike their Romany counter-part. Romanies used these 'Burtons', but mostly bought second-hand. In most cases, Romanies would not have a 'Burton' wagon made new.

Now to wagon number four, the 'Bowtop'. This wagon is Romany through and through. It is also the lightest of the four wagons and its only downside is that it's a little dark and gloomy inside, having only one back window. This wagon was very popular with North Country Romanies in hill terrain. No other wagon will beat it. Reader, to see a 'Bowtop' in all its glory you must see one made by that legend of a wagon maker, Bill Wright of Haigh in Yorkshire. It's the Rolls-Royce of wagons.

Another fairly recent type is the 'Open Lot' or 'Yorkshire Bow'. Most of these are made by Romanies themselves. It's a fairly simple canvas top put on a 'Bradford' trolley or a 'Lambeth' dray and is used today for Romanies to attend horse fairs.

There is another wagon...or maybe I must state, there used to be another wagon, but it is thought that like the Dodo bird it is now extinct. It was a monster of a wagon, called a 'Brush wagon' or sometimes called a 'Fen' wagon. It differed greatly from all the other wagons which I have described. It was a mobile *shobi*. It was used mostly by Broom Squires, as they were known, and also Tiger Hunters – people who sold rugs...hence Tiger Rugs. Some were Romanies, but most would be *posh-rats* (half bloods). The large 'Fen' wagons had racks, hooks and cupboards fixed to the outside. The large roof racks were used to display and hold stuff: mostly brooms, brushes, pots, pans and carpets. The 'Fen' wagon had its door on the back, not on the front.

How long does a Romany *vardo* last for? Being used each day, if a good wagon is looked after well, it will last as long as a set of *stackus* (teeth). To have a good wagon made back in the day would cost you in the region of £100 to £125, depending on how much inter rib carving you had. You could at the same time buy a secondhand old wagon for £50. My old grandfather, Butty Lamb, had his last 'Reading' wagon made by Leonards of Soham in Cambridgeshire, which I think cost about £100. It was still being used, not on the *tober*, but as a home for Butty's *mort* Mary-Ann and her son Winks Lamb up to about the 1950s at Catch-Pit Lane in North Walsham. Today you still hear people saying, "We have a Romany *vardo* that is 150 years old." They are talking rubbish – a wagon is mostly made from pine timber and if it is used daily on the tober, it will not last more than 50 years.

NORTH WALSHAM ALL-SORTS

I told you that my uncle, Winks Lamb, lived at Catch-Pit Lane. After the wagon got a little on the rough side, Winks bought himself a wooden shed to live in. He also bought himself a Dansette portable radio. Winks was in his hut one day and outside his *puv* on the *drom* stood a TV and radio detector van. Winks had his radio on, listening to Desert Island Discs, when he spotted the van. Instead of turning his radio off, Winks threw it onto the floor of his hut and kicked it, jumping on it until it was dead! After Winks had told me about this, I said, "Why did you not just turn it off? They would not have been able to detect it." When Winks bought his next radio, he was down at the old post office to get a licence as fast as he could! There's some funny old boys about.

Talking about living in a hut, I can tell you a better one than that. Over at Sloley near Worstead, Winks and I went to see an old *Gorgio* to buy a bit of *rust* from him. The old *gilly* (man) had a large, rough old field, which was covered in stinging nettles. He kept a few *baulos* (pigs) which he was fattening. If my memory is correct, and I think it is, his name was Whitleton. Winks and I walked onto his old *puv* and shouted, "Are you about, Master?" No reply! So we drew a little further in and shouted again, and out of one of the roughest old wooden sheds I have ever seen came this old *mush*. He never had a door on the old shed; all he had was an old sack hanging down and a bale of *pus* (straw) at the bottom. Out he came. Christ, he looked a mess; he was living in the old shed with a rough old Collie dog. The old *mush* stank like an old dead coypu rat. I think we bought a bit of *rust* from him. Did he *pen and ink* (stink)! Years ago there were plenty of old boys about like him who would *sove* (sleep) anywhere.

Back to North Walsham! Talking about Winks and his poor old *dai* (mother), let's see if I can find a few more old characters who frequented this old town of North Walsham. I will travel back and try and tell you of some of the early ones, and then we can come down into more recent times. That's if there are any still left. They don't make them like they did! Christ, this old writing is boring, but it's better than sitting in my front room with my old gal! She sits there for hours watching Coronation Street and Eastenders on that old telly. It's a wonder she can still see out of her *yoks* with all the television.

Sod Coronation Street – I am going to take you down Vicarage Street in North Walsham. We will meet some real characters – more interesting than Ken Barlow! Vicarage Street is where Cory Brown lived. His real name was Freddy Brown. He had his fingers in more pies than Simple Simon. I mentioned Cory in my last book; all this writing is driving me up the wall. But back to Cory…he used to put up all the market stalls on a Thursday for the town council. He also had his own stall on the market place, selling *mass* (meat) for *juks* (dogs). Cory was also a bookie's runner for Bill Juby, the local bookmaker. Cory would collect all the bets from the pubs in North Walsham that punters had left there. In Vicarage Street, where he lived, it was all little houses with hardly any gardens. Cory had some bantams he wanted to *fence* so he got a punter to come and have a deal. The buyer was not too impressed with Cory's bantams and told Cory so. Cory quickly replied, "The best bantams are roosting up the trees," it being of a night time. He added, "they are lovely birds." Cory got the *mush* to part with his *loover*. Cory told him to come back the next day and he would have the better bantams from the *rookers* (trees). The next day, he came for his bantams and realised that there are no trees in Vicarage Street. Cory had tucked the old *gilly* up. Cory also had a piece of marshland on the outskirts of the town. Cory would store up scrap and he had a large heap on the marsh. He once chased my mates and I from it when we were just boys. We did not know that scrap was Cory's. I think if he had caught us he would have *mullered* us.

Let me think: who else is there in the old town? Let's not forget Spuddy Edwards, who operated down Catch-Pit Lane in North Walsham. Spuddy would be at the Irelands' Park Lane sale every Thursday buying *kanis* (chickens) and *shooshis* (rabbits). Most were dressed out and dispatched to Smithfield Market in London. Spuddy had a brother called Ernie Edwards. He had a blacksmith's shop in Mitre Tavern yard, but sadly all these old places and people are long gone. What a sad shame. Talking about livestock dealers, Ikey Wright from North Walsham, Malcolm Oliver and Tom Medler from Hevingham, and Reggie Bell (one of old Cockle Bell's boys) would all be at the North Walsham saleground on a Thursday. These old dealing boys would do what is known as 'standing in'. They would share out the pens of *kanis* and *shooshis*, paying only a little per pen. After a while, Billy King, Irelands' auctioneer would say, "Let's have a pen of these chickens or rabbits for the paper!" The dealers would then bid up this pen. Each week in the local Eastern Daily Press you would have a market report telling readers what livestock at local markets was making. So, in fact, this was a false report because only one pen of each livestock made this high price. It also encouraged people to bring their livestock to North Walsham sale and get these high prices – some hope! All the rest of the livestock was being nearly *monged* by Spuddy Edwards and his conspirators. This was the way things were done. You could not blame these old dealers; they just liked getting their heads together, if you know what I mean. Reader, never believe all that you read in a newspaper.

Ikey Wright – Christ, was he a character. The secret with Ikey was to never get involved with him or he would rope you in like Roy Rodgers, the cowboy. Ikey hired a few pieces of land around here along with his son, Billy Wright. They did a little farming around these parts. Ikey would place adverts in the Exchange & Mart advertising for all sorts of chickens, pigeons, dogs, rabbits, ferrets...you name it, Ikey was your man! I think if you wanted an elephant Ikey would have found you one! Ikey would often sell up front. What this means is Ikey got his money first and then went looking for the goods. Ikey also worked on Irelands' sales. They had one here in North Walsham on a Thursday, Reepham on a Wednesday and Holt on a Friday, so old Ikey was kept busy. Ikey came after me one day, and he said, "I have got a little job for you, Mike." Since I knew what Ikey was like, I said,

"What job have you got me?"

"Well," Ikey said, "an old *striker* (donkey) of mine has broken out of its field and has got in with Jane Lewis's horses at Bacton Wood Farm. The old gal's going mad: give me a hand to catch it?"

Here we go, I thought – another Ikey Wright scheme. Up to Bacton Wood Farm Ikey and I went in his old truck. F**k me! I have seen newer things on Antiques Roadshow. We would be lucky if we got there…what a bit of *kinder* (shit). We arrived at the *puv* and out stepped Ikey. "How are we going to catch that old *striker*?" I said to Ikey. Bear in mind that it did not have a halter on it and it looked like an evil old bastard. Ikey said, "Go into the field, Mike, and run after it. When you get beside it, throw your arms around its neck and pull it down. The old *striker* is as weak as piss."

Ikey must have thought I was John Wayne. It seemed to me that that old *striker* could have pulled the Houses of Parliament down. I thought to myself, "I better put up a show and try to catch it." So I ran across the *puv* after the old striker. Christ, could that old bastard run. I was nearly f*****d, but I managed to throw my arms around its neck. I was hanging on for dear life underneath its neck. I knew I was on a loser. In fact, as soon as I met Ikey Wright, I was a loser! I had to let go: I hit the turf and the old *striker* ran over top of me! It pressed me so hard with its hooves that as I laid there on the *puv* (ground), I pissed myself. Ikey cried, "Get up, Mike, and try again." I said, "F**k you, Ikey

Wright. You have a go, you minge. You said that old *striker* was as weak as piss! I don't know about you, but I'm covered in piss and I am going home. Catch the *striker* yourself." There were some funny old boys.

Ikey had turned out an old Hereford cow on a marsh down here on the common. She had a calf and then a second one. The first-born calf grew up into a large animal, staying with its mother and younger sister. These three animals had very large horns and they were semi wild. Ikey just left them to grow up on the old marsh. When the first heifer got to a certain age, you could claim money from the Ministry, but you had to have the animal tagged. So one evening in the summertime, Ikey rounded up a gang of us to round up the wild heifer. To begin with, the operation went smoothly, but as you know – nothing goes smoothly with Ikey Wright. We managed to separate it from its mother and drive it into Ikey's small farm yard. Down at the bottom of the yard stood little Ronnie Warnes, a fellow who worked for Ikey. His job was to stop the heifer, and then we would drive it into Ikey's shed. Ikey shouted to Ronnie, "Stand your ground and stop it." Well, this wild mad Hereford put its horns down and tossed poor Ronnie up into the heavens and he hit the deck. I think he cracked two ribs. It then ran straight through a thick dense hedge like it was not there, leaving a hole in the hedge the same shape as itself. Ikey's gang pursued it over some fields and finally we lost it in the middle of Witton woods. By then it was getting dark. We decided we would return the next night.

The next night the gang returned – there were about 7 or 8 of us. At last we found the heifer and turned it back towards Ikey's farm. The farm was very near to the old canal, and we had almost gotten her into the farm when she was off again. This time she jumped into the muddy canal and laid there. We tried every means to get her out. We were all wet and covered in mud. After a time, she jumped up and was off again, and this time she ran almost a mile to Marshgate House where Ikey lived, where the same thing happened. This time it was Jack Pooley, Ikey's son-in-law, who was the one who tried to stop her. She tossed Jack up into the air and nearly *mullered* him. Then she ran almost back to the canal where she turned into Cyril Bell's scrap yard near the canal. We opened a shed door and it ran in. Thank goodness for that. Ikey was sick as a pig; he almost gave the Hereford to Cyril Bell. The next day Cyril got a cattle float to take it to an abattoir. The float backed up to the door, and the Hereford walked up onto the float as quiet as a lamb.

*

Another character in North Walsham was Mick Wilkins. Mick and his old mother lived in a large old house on the Norwich Road. Mick dealt in bicycles and he sold hundreds of them. Mick and his mother also had a fruit and vegetable round and they would travel around to nearby villages selling their produce. Mick had a trailer which he towed behind his bike. I remember in the early Sixties when I first started dealing in antiques, I called around their big old house. Mick and his mother had the first colour TV around here. It was a big one...the only trouble was that they had gotten short of *loover* and had sold the table that the TV stood on. They had to watch the TV with it on the floor. I bought some nice *covels* from them. It was not too long before Mick sold most of the stuff in the house. In the Sixties there were 13 pubs in the centre of North Walsham. Every night, Mick Wilkins would have a lager and lime in every pub. In the end they let themselves go and got very dirty. They lost the big house and I think they finished up down at Cromer.

Billy Taylor, known as Squiggles, was my father's mate, though he would rob a workhouse child. Each Saturday night, Edgie and Squiggles would go out drinking. They also had a bit of rivalry going on between them. Anyway, Edgie spotted in a local shop in the town a nice silk brown *diklo* (scarf) with white spots, so he took the plunge and bought it. He told Mother, "I have done Squiggles Taylor when I meet him in The Anchor on Saturday night." Mother decided she would play a trick on Edgie. She went to the same shop and bought another scarf and gave it to Squiggles, unknown to Edgie. Come Saturday night, Edgie was preening himself up. Up to The Anchor he went. He opened the door and walked in and there sat Squiggles. He cried out to Edgie, "You have got my scarf on!" Christ, was Edgie savage. He said, "That *sube juk* (f**k dog) Taylor had a scarf on just like mine!" It was weeks before Edgie got over it.

Here is a quick tale about Edgie. Late on a Thursday, when Edgie would come from the market, it would mostly be on his old woman's bike. However, if he had bought something at the market, he would be in his old horse-drawn pig float. This was a high-sided cart to hold animals. Anyway, David Woodhouse was standing near his gate on Rolfs Corner on the common. Down Manor Road came Edgie's old float. The old *tit* was getting a move on, and round Rolfs Corner it came. When David looked, there we no one driving it. He thought, "Where's Edgie?" He thought it was a ghost cart. It was not a ghost cart; Edgie was there, laying in the bottom of the old float, sleeping beside a large white sow. Edgie was as *motty* (drunk) as a *juk*. The old *tit* knew the way home. Good job it did!

*

Here is another tale concerning Edgie. In his later years, Edgie had a heart condition and was told to take things easy and not to put himself under any stress. About two miles outside North Walsham at Swafield was a nice little *kitchema* called The Dukes Head. On a Saturday night we would take Edgie down there so he could play cards with the landlady and a handful of customers. Edgie, just before closing time, would catch a bus outside The Dukes Head and get off the bus in North Walsham, have a *shant* with us in North Walsham, and then we would take him home. One Saturday night, Edgie stepped onto the bus to North Walsham. Edgie was the only passenger on the bus. After a time, Edgie said to the bus driver, "You are a long while getting to North Walsham!" The driver said, "We have already stopped at North Walsham – we are nearly at Coltishall." The next stop would have been Norwich. The driver stopped and let Edgie off, and he walked all the way back to North Walsham. We always thought this was the demise of Edgie, because just after that he suffered a severe stroke which finished him off. Bless him. We asked him why he didn't see the lights in North Walsham when the bus stopped, and Edgie replied, "The bloody windows were steamed up!"

*

Today I am writing this book under a shady tree in my garden behind my *kenner*. It's a scorcher for late August. The *chiriclos* (birds) are singing in the *rookers* and it's a grand day to be alive and kicking in old Mother England's *puvs*. Unfortunately, today I have just received some bad news from my old friend Dennis Hatch from Norwich. His father was old Sam Hatch (Tighty Hatch). Dennis told me his oldest brother, Freddy Hatch, had *mullered*. Now, here we have a character of the first degree. Freddy, like his two brothers Dennis and Malcolm, were true Norwichers. It is much the same as a cockney, who is very distinct from a Londoner. A proper Norwicher is much sharper and more fly than other Norfolk people, but a true Norwicher is not only sharp and at times very imposing – he is also kind and generous. A better person you would fail to find. Back to Freddy, though. Reader, you most probably never met Freddy. Your loss! I will try to describe him. Freddy was on the small size, with a pleasing *mui* (face). He had the looks of Steve McQueen, the late actor, with very sharp piercing *yoks*. On meeting him, you would know he was not the sort to try and take advantage of.

So there I was, standing on Stalham sale ground on a Tuesday in the Sixties, ready to see if I was going to take some good *loover* for the *covels* I had put into the sale when along comes Freddy. This small wiry Steve McQueen lookalike and I got *rokkering*, and as we stood there, two mouthy Norwichers came up to Freddy and started to give him grief. The *mush* with the big *mui* (mouth) was a guy by the name of Curly. I think he used to buy up low grade antiques. He had a bit of muscle with him,. He looked like he had come out of Planet of the Apes. Apparently Curly had a bit of grief with Freddy and the two were getting ready for a *chingren* (fight). Freddy, despite his small stature, stood his ground and said to Curly, "I have been in your *gaff* (house) several times and I have never seen any Lonsdale belts or trophies on your shelves. Another thing, Curly, if you are good at fighting, don't do it for nothing. You can earn good *loover*. But seeing as you two toe rags want to have a go, let's go up on the car park and I will take you both on!" They both stood and stared at Freddy in dismay and they both realised they had picked on the wrong man! They slunk off like the *juks* that they were. One more thing. Freddy, wherever you are now...it was a privilege to have known you. Rest in peace, and no *cooring* (fighting) up there! I will be there one day and I like a quiet time.

Another strange old character from these parts was Archie Sutton. He deserves a mention. Archie was a tall man. Always wearing a battered old trilby hat, he wore glasses and rode an old sit up and beg bike. It was said that he came from a well to do family. The first mention I heard of him was that he lived in an old steel lifeboat down on the river at Honing. The old boat was still there a few years ago. Word has it that during the last war, a German plane dropped a few bombs near Archie's boat and Archie made a quick retreat from the boat. Next time I caught up with him, he was living down at Little London near North Walsham in a small cottage in a nice peaceful location. Then Archie thought he would do a little restoration to the cottage. He thought that if he made his cottage smaller he would not pay such high rates. Archie pulled down the top of the cottage, made it into a bungalow and replaced the tiled roof with tin roofing sheets and in this hovel Archie resided. Archie spent most of his life in bookies offices, mostly in Bill Juby's in North Walsham. Archie compiled his own form book. When Archie did pick a winner, he had only placed a shilling on it. Sometimes he would occasionally do a little casual work: the odd day on a threshing drum or maybe hoeing a few farmers' sugar beet. I met up again with Archie in 1966. My uncle, Winks Lamb, and I were down at Worstead factory working on the pea vining machines. Archie was there. I think the factory gave Archie a light job, but the trouble with Archie was he never *scranned* himself too well and he was always on the weak side. I remember him well down there. He would have for his lunch and dinner a tin or two of tinned cat food and no hot drink. Archie would drink straight out of a tap! On this site all the water was recycled and not to be drunk. It did not bother Archie! Sadly, like so many characters, he has gone.

*

I cannot finish this book without mentioning Tommy Manes from Mundesley. He was a real diamond. I think I am right in saying that Tommy, like me, lived in a railway carriage at Charlie Payne's farm at Mundesley. Charlie and his son Chris were very fond of Tommy. Tommy got his living mostly with his old *gridler* (bike) which had a small grindstone attached on the handlebars. Tommy would put the old bike up on its stand, and pedal and sharpen people's *catches* (scissors) and *churis* (knives). This was known in the Romany world as a *churi-mengro* (knife grinder). He called his old *treader* (bike) his 'wheel of fortune'. Always being around folks' *kairs* working, he would buy up antiques. He was very knowledgeable about antiques, but if myself or any other dealer happened to call at Tommy's *kair* he would always sell you something, always leaving a little meat on the bones for you. This means Tommy would let you buy it right so you could earn out of it.

Tommy left the railway carriage and moved into a bungalow in Mundesley. I did not know Tommy's son, but his daughter, Dorothy, who Tommy called 'Topsy', was in my class at school. She still lives in Mundesley with her husband Peter; they are a lovely couple. Tommy, sadly, did not pass away peacefully. He was killed in a roadside accident at Paston near where he lived. Each year, Tommy would send out lots of Christmas cards to friends. I would receive one in early December, and I knew it was from Tommy because it would be the first one.

I mentioned that Tommy dealt in antiques. I think I better give you a round up of antique dealers I have dealt with in this area. Leslie Pead from Aylsham was the top man for lower grade shipping furniture. He shipped mostly to the USA. A nicer man you would not find. Gordon Dixon, another Aylsham man, for a time shipped furniture with Leslie Pead. I remember taking Gordon to view some furniture in the Sixties when the person who we were trying to buy it from said, "I have someone else trying to view it." Gordon in his very brash way said, "I don't care if you have Arthur Negus coming to look at it, Gordon Dixon is here now." Mike Hicks from Stalham Antiques gallery was also a very strong buyer in the trade. Mike to this day still trades in bespoke antiques. I could, if I wished, fill up plenty more pages with buyers of a smaller nature, who, like myself, used to work the knocker. That's the hardest way to buy antiques but one of the most rewarding. The boys on the knocker were at the bottom of the chain, but without us there would not have been so much trade. When a person on the knocker buys something, it's fresh. It has not been hauled around sale grounds; these are genuine, untouched antiques which dealers love. None of these buyers would ever aspire to get wealthy because we bought today and sold tomorrow, taking a small, quick profit and starting the cycle all over again the very next day.

Over at Wood Dalling, near Reepham, lived Jack Ellis. He would buy up a fair amount of old antique furniture. For a number of years, Jack was selling Barley Twist oak tables to a young dealer for about £10 a pop. This went on for a year or so until, one day, Jack dropped into Aylsham sale and saw that these oak tables were selling for £30 each. He went mad! When his young buyer came around again, Jack said to him, "You dirty little toe rag! You have been robbing me blind for years!" Another good old operator was Bert Eastoe from Norwich. He was on the knocker for years and had his own shop in Norwich. Also there were Dennis Hatch and his brother Malcolm Hatch. Dennis exported large quantities of bespoke antiques to France and Australia. There were also the Stanley family from Wymondham, who mostly bought from sales and auctions. Sid Cramer and his sons from Rackheath Hall were good buyers, too, as was Rodney Pratt from South Walsham. Old Brewster from Saxthorpe would supply USA airmen from Sculthorpe mostly with large furniture. Out near Bungay was Harry Adams. He was a strong buyer at a sale; Harry would not stop for anyone. If he wanted it, Harry would buy it.

Some Closing Words

Well, Reader, that's about it! I cannot keep writing forever; I will run out of paper. It's now about time that I come to a close with this book. Let's just pause for a moment and have a reflection of how things are now. All the true old characters, I think, have passed away. What have we got left? Most Romanies I still know just do not want to talk about the past. They all have been brought up in a different world. They don't dress like Romanies and they certainly don't talk Romany. None of them know of places like Grimston Common or Thetford Common. These places were our home - our own domain. We were kings and queens of the commons.

In writing this book, I hope I have shown you the way it was and have given you a sense of direction so you may instil in your children and in theirs the ways of the old Romanies. Once more, I will repeat again, there's a time and a place for everything and everything has its day. For the true Romany, that day has sadly come. I think it reached its zenith in the early 19th Century, and then around the 1940s the decline began. Today, we only have fond memories of a great and spontaneous race of people. There are still a few isolated pockets of Romanies still trying to hang on to their inner beliefs and traditions, but how much longer can they survive? I will tell you one thing; they will resist and not give in. This I know for sure. We have survived for over a thousand years. Maybe, just maybe, they will succeed in their inspirations and dreams to keep alive their traditions and heritage to hand down to future generations. Just before I close down the last page of this book, a strange and wonderful thing occurred a few moments ago. My phone rang, and when I picked it up and listened, a Romany lady spoke to me. Apparently she had just been given my book *Kaka Rokker Romany* by her daughter. This fine Romany lady lives somewhere down south near Bournemouth. She was so pleased to have read my book, which she had enjoyed very much. This lady told me she is 90 years old and is related to the Romany families of Coopers and Smiths. As we talked, I had a lump in my throat – to think this lovely Romany lady had gotten so much enjoyment from my book. This lady has made my task of writing so worthwhile. To know that I was talking to a true Romany lady, hundreds of miles away...that has indeed made my day. Thank you, *rinkeni Romany rawnie*.

After this book, I don't know where the next will come from. I have mostly covered all the old characters that I have known, and there are none left. Maybe I will write a book on wagon life in days gone by. It will be part fiction and part non-fiction, and it will deal with wagon life here in Norfolk. I know of plenty old Romanies and their way of life, so it should make good reading. Plus, it would show younger Romanies what their elders had to endure: the struggle to eke out a living. How they managed to survive through hard times. Yes, I think there is room for this, but right now I must close the old *vardo* door and get ready again for the *drom* and hope to inspire you to read and understand the Romany culture which has almost slipped away from us. Let's all cling on and keep spreading the *lav*.

Mike Harmer

August 2019

Glossary

The Romany Chal word book.
The spelling of these words is phonetic.
English and cockney slang is generally indicated in brackets.

A

Amber nectar (slang)	Beer

B

Bait (Old English word)	Feed
Bal	Hair
Bar	Pound
Barvalo	Rich
Barvello rye	Rich gentleman
Baulo	Pig
Beng	Devil
Bewer	Woman
Bin (slang)	Wallet
Bitti	Little
Blue	To sell
Blued	Sold
Boat race (slang)	Face
Bokra engro	Shepherd
Bokra mush	Shepherd
Boo	Stove
Bor	Hedge
Bosh	Violin

Bowler	Wheel
Bowlers	Wheels
Bricks (slang)	Houses
Bung (slang)	To pay
Buty	Work

C

Call	To sell
Calling	Selling
Cambori	Pregnant
Cas	Hay
Catches	Scissors
Chad	Arse
Chal	Boy
Chats	Things
Chavies	Children, kids
Chavo	Child
Chaw	Grass
Chib	Tongue
Chie	Girl
Ching	To fight
Chingaripen	Argument, row
Chingaro	Quarrel, fight
Chiriclo	Bird
Chiv (slang)	Blade
Chokkers	Shoes, boots
Choomer	Kiss
Chop	Deal
Chor	Food

Chore	To steal
Chori	Poor
Churi	Knife
Churi-mengro	Knife-grinder
Churis	Knives
Claret (slang)	Blood
Clod (slang)	Coin
Congri	Church
Coor	To fight
Cooramengro	Boxer
Coorapen	Fight
Coover	Thing
Coroengro	Blacksmith
Cosh (slang)	Wood
Costies	Sticks
Covels	Things
Curlo	Throat
Cushni	Basket
Cushni mengro	Basket-maker
Custi	Good
Custi bok	Good luck
Custi rarde	Good night
Custi rye	Good man

D

Dadrus	Father
Dai	Mother
Dass	Cup
Delomescro	Hammer

Desh	Ten
Dik	Look
Dik	To see
Diking	Looking
Diklo	Scarf
Dilly (slang)	Cart
Ding	Throw
Dinolo	Fool
Divvus	Day
Divvuski conger	School
Divvy	Silly
Dovel	God
Drag (slang)	Car, cart
Draw	Go
Drom	Road
Drop	To poison
Drover	Man who drives animals
Dui	Two
Dui and dass	Cups and saucers
Duis of peava	Cup of tea
Dukkering	Fortune telling
Dukkering	Telling fortunes

F

Fake	To mend, to make
Faked	Mended, made
Fawnee	Ring
Fence (slang)	Sell

Flat mush	Non-romany pretending to be romany
Fly (slang)	Sharp
Fly mush	Sharp man
Fonga	Fork

G

Gaff (slang)	House
Gavver	Policeman
Gilly	Man
Ginger beer shop (slang)	Pub
Givengro	Farmer
Glazer (slang)	Window
Gorgio	Non-romany
Grai	Horse
Gran	Barn
Gridler	Bike
Gridler	Street singer
Groovni	Cow
Guero	Man
Gunner	Sack
Guvenii	Cow

H

Hatch	Stop
Hatch	To stop, to stay
Hatching	Stopping
Hatching tan	Stopping place
Hawk (slang)	Sell

Herri	Leg
Hindity	Dirty
Holeno	Landlord
Holler (slang)	Shout
Holofer	Sock
Hotchi-witchi	Hedgehog
Hotchimengri	Frying pan

I

Ivory (slang)	Teeth

J

Jam jar (slang)	Car
Jam-jar (slang)	Glass of beer
Jell	To go
Jelling	Going
John bradburys (slang)	Pound notes
Joobs	Fleas
Juk	Dog
Juva	Girl

K

Kair	House
Kak-looverd	Penniless
Kani	Chicken
Kas	Hay
Kaulo	Black
Kaulo ratti	Black blood
Kaun	Ear
Kaun-fawnees	Ear-rings
Kekauvi	Kettle

Kekubi	Kettle
Kenner	House
Kettering costies	Gathering wood
Kin	To buy
Kinder	Shit
Kipsi	Basket
Kissi-doris	Purse strings
Kitchema	Pub
Kitchema mengro	Landlord
Kite wagon	Tall kite shaped wagon
Knits (slang)	Woollens
Knocker (slang)	Buying antiques from houses
Kooli	Soldier
Koro	Cup

L

Lark liner	Smallest lining brush
Lav	Word
Lav chingaripen	Argument
Lel	To take
Lil	Book
Livnoker	Pub
Lollo	Copper
Loover	Money
Lubnies	Ladies of the night

M

Marine store	Rag shop
Mass	Meat

Massengro	Butcher
Matchko	Cat
Maul	Wood club used in peg making
Mell	To not pay
Melled	Not paid for
Miltog	Shirt
Minditsi	Virgin
Minge (slang)	C**t
Moll (slang)	Loose woman
Monesta	Woman
Mong	To beg
Monging	Begging
Monista	Woman of ill repute
Moody	To kid, to joke
Morro	Bread
Mort	Woman/wife
Motty	Drunk
Moulder	Lorry
Mui	Face, mouth
Mulleno hev	Grave
Muller	To die
Mullo	The dead
Mumper	Half-blood
Mumper mush	Gorgio man
Mush	Man, fellow
Mush (slang)	Umbrella
Musker	Policeman

Mutra	Pee, piss

N

Naflinken	Hospital
Narky (slang)	Bad tempered
Nav (plural: naviour)	Name
Needi	Traveller
Niksas	Nothing
Nongo	Naked
Nook	Penny

O

O dordi	Oh dear

P

Pani	Water
Patteran	Trail of leaves
Peava	Tea
Pen and ink (slang)	Stink
Pester	To pay
Pestered	Paid
Petul	Horseshoe
Pire	Feet
Poknie	Magistrate
Porengripen	Writing
Posh	Half
Posh-rat	Half-blood
Pralas	Brothers
Punter (slang)	Customer
Puro	Old
Purodaia	Old mother

Purodia	Grandmother
Pus	Straw
Putsi	Pocket
Puv	Field
Puved	Put horse in field
Puvengro	Potato
Pygtle	Norfolk name meaning small field

R

Rakla	Woman
Rap	To swear
Rap fawnees	Silver rings
Rarde	Night
Rarti	Night
Ratler (slang)	Train
Ratti	Blood
Rawnee	Girl
Rinkeni	Pretty
Rinkeni monista	Pretty woman
Rokers	Trees
Rokker	To talk
Rom	Husband
Rom	To marry
Rooker	Tree
Rust (slang)	Scrap
Rye	Gentleman

S

Saster	Iron

Saster kaba cosh	Iron kettle hook
Scimish	Beer, drink, to drink
Scran	Food, to eat
Shant	Pint of beer
Sharps	Shafts (on a wagon)
Sherbert (slang)	Beer
Shero	Head
Shobi	Shop
Shohorry	Shilling
Shooshi	Rabbit
Sider	Horse tied beside another horse on a wagon
Skimish	To drink
Sky (slang)	Parson
Smoothing	Fishing
Smut	Brass
Snorkel	Swede
Sonneco	Gold
Sove	Sleep, to sleep
Soving	Sleeping
Stackus	Teeth
Stakas	Teeth
Stiff	To arrest
Stiffed	Arrested
Stigur	Door/gate
Stir (slang)	Prison
Stirapen	Prison
Straps	Harness

Striker (slang)	Donkey
Sube-juk	F**g dog
Sunakai	Gold
Swegglers	Pipes
Swegler	Pipe

T

Tan	Place, tent
Tat shop (slang)	Marine store
Tatra mengri	Frying pan
Tats (slang)	Rags
Tatting	Collecting old rags
Thrashed	Frightened
Tiblo	Cigarette
Ticker (slang)	Heart
Tit (slang)	Female horse
Titfa	Hat
Tober	Road
Togram	Linen peg
Togs (slang)	Clothes
Tom foolery (slang)	Jewellery
Tootchi	Breast
Touch (slang)	Result
Tova	Smoke
Trailer	Caravan
Treader	Bike
Trouble and strife (slang)	Wife
Tud	Milk

Turnpike sailor (slang)	Tramp
Tuv	Smoke, tobacco
Twilers	Trousers

V

Vangus	Finger
Vardo	Wagon
Vast	Hand
Vonger	Money

W

Wafti	Bad
Wardo	Cart
Waspy (slang)	Sharp
Wasts	Hands
Wellgorus	Fair
Wonger	Money
Woodrus	Bed

Y

Yog	Fire
Yogged	Burnt
Yogger	Gun
Yogger mush	Gamekeeper
Yok	Eye
Yoro	Egg

Acknowledgements

First and foremost without Nick White's encouragements and tireless endeavours to get this humble book published, it would have remained a heap of unfinished notes. Thank you, Nick. Also to Kate Anderson in the west country who kindly put my somewhat indifferent writings into a readable form.

I am also indebted to my lovely niece Glenda Curtis from Briston for her forensic secretarial contributions, translating my handwritten scrawl from hieroglyphics to recognisable English.

Last, but by no means, least my *mort*, Hazel Jane, for having to endure living with a "Mush" who spends more time with his books then he does with her.

Thanks every one.

About the Author

Mike Harmer was born in a railway carriage in 1942 at Spa Common. He still lives on the same site in a *kair* he had built in 1990. He had three sisters and one brother. All but his youngest sister, Maureen, have passed away. He still runs his reclamation business and lends a hand to his son, Rodney, in his joinery business.

The Romany Chal is Mike's second book. His first, *Kaka, Rokker Romany* was published in 2019 and there are a further two awaiting finishing touches. He claims that one day he might retire when The Grim Reaper comes looking for him, but, until then, he is still up the *tober* looking for something *custi* to buy.